Cakes, Desserts and Puddings

Amandine's recipes

Cakes, Desserts and Puddings

Photography by Akiko Ida

Baking cakes at home is a pleasure we can all enjoy. This book is a collection of very easy recipes remembered with affection from my childhood in France: pure butter brioche, Swiss roll, spice cake, madeleines, yogurt cakes and so on. Maybe you remember sampling such delicacies while on holiday in France.

Here you'll find the traditional methods, together with some special tips to help you produce the real thing using recipes handed down from one generation to the next. With three times nothing, a little butter, some flour and eggs, French mothers and grandmothers knew how to create what they wanted – langues de chat, choux pastry puffs, chocolate charlotte, tarte Tatin, pound cake, fruit cake, cherry clafoutis, apple turnovers and so on.

If you can't get hold of the exact ingredients, you can easily replace certain items with ones from your own store cupboard. The fruit breads, tarts and cakes all work well with good quality ingredients.

Amandine

MEASUREMENTS

Please note that metric and imperial measurements do not correspond exactly. Therefore use either metric or imperial measurements when following a recipe, not both.

Guide to home baking

TINS FOR ALL OCCASIONS Four or five tins are all you need to make about 90 per cent of the cakes in this book – that's all! Preferably they should be nonstick tins to make life easier. Never use a fork or knife to release your cake from the tin. You are likely to spoil both your cake and your tin if you do.

Choosing the right tin

Keep to simple tins: one loaf tin and one round sandwich tin 22 cm (about 9 inches) in diameter will be sufficient to make many delicious cakes. You can gradually acquire more sophisticated tins as you need them.

Caring for your tins

Take care never to scratch the surface with an abrasive sponge and do not use strong cleaning products. Certain nonstick tins are dishwasher proof. When you buy them they will have a label telling you if they are.

Tart tins

These can be made of ovenproof porcelain or metal and come in many shapes and sizes. You can ring the changes!

Gratin dishes

A standard gratin dish can be used for clafoutis and flans. To clean off stubborn stains put a few tablespoonfuls of bicarbonate of soda in the base and fill it two-thirds full of warm water. Put it in the oven for about twenty minutes. It will come out sparkling.

Fruit cake (bread) tins

There is a secret to a successful fruit cake: put the tin on a baking tray on a shelf in your oven. This will prevent the base from burning during cooking and the cake will be cooked to perfection.
To see if it is cooked sufficiently plunge a knife blade into the middle – if nothing sticks to it, the cake is done.

Deep, round tins

The ideal diameter for most of the cakes in this book is 22 cm (about 9 inches). Some tins are spring-form (see opposite page) – they are generally used for home-made breads and buns. Use these tins for cheesecakes and delicate cakes that are difficult to release. Never use a spring-form tin for runny or fatty mixtures which may leak out during cooking.

Brioche tins

Used for baking brioches and Kougelhopfs. There is a wide range of such tins available in Alsace – should you go there! You can sometimes find them in old-fashioned ironmonger's shops and in specialized shops selling baking equipment.

SMALL UTENSILS Here are a few practical items that will help you succeed with your home-made pastries. They are not essential but they will serve you well.

Rolling pin

Ideal for preparing home-made pastry. Usually made of wood, there are two kinds: professional rolling pins sometimes come without handles but they are more than 35 cm (14 inches) long. Not a fraction of the pastry is wasted! The more usual kind has two handles.

Cake rack

Made of stainless steel, a cake rack is the best way to let your cakes 'rest' after cooking. You could also use it for serving your cakes at the table. It lends a nostalgic air.

Brushes

Use small ones for brushing over your tarts and cakes. Those made of natural fibres are preferable. Professional equipment shops and some ironmongers sell special pastry brushes. To clean them just hold them under running water but don't forget to dry them.

Biscuit cutters

Use these for tartlets and to give a different look to buns and biscuits.

Spatulas

The ones with a rubber blade are best. They mean that none of your mixture is wasted.

Pastry wheels

Made of wood or stainless steel, these are generally used for making ravioli. You can also use them for crafting interesting shapes with your left-over shortcrust or puff pastry. Essential for making Linzertorte (see page 122).

Piping nozzles and bags

Used for creamy or frothy mixtures. Made of fabric or nylon, the bags are flexible and respond to the slightest pressure of the finger. You need a little practice. Different shaped nozzles will enable you to decorate your cakes attractively.

Balloon whisk

The alternative to an electric beater. It is however more practical, being ideal for making emulsions and for folding sugar into whites of egg. Choose a strong stainless steel version. The metal wires should be supple but firm.

rolling pins
racks
brushes
spatulas
wheels
nozzles
whisks

Flours

Plain flour

This is the flour commonly used for making cakes and biscuits. It is a wheat flour (usually variety 45) – an ideal flour that is found everywhere.

Self-raising flour

White wheat flour to which salt and baking powder have been added.

Chestnut flour

This traditional flour used in cakes and biscuits in the centre of France or Corsica will give a delicious hint of chestnut flavour to your desserts.

Maize flour

This yellow flour low in gluten but rich in starch is perfect for making polenta, puddings, pancakes and certain cakes such as lemon and almond cake.

Buckwheat flour

Low in gluten, this flour is mainly used to make Breton 'galettes' and certain types of pancake.

TIP • You should always sieve your flour when you make a cake to get rid of any lumps and make sure your mixture is smooth.

Different types of sugar

There are two main sorts of sugar: beet sugar and cane sugar. Both can be used in baking.
Sugar is used to sweeten desserts but it also raises the acidity of certain fruits, colours cakes in the cooking process, lends a firm consistency to certain recipes (meringues for instance) and, of course, is used for decoration (as in royal icing, icing sugar or spun sugar).

Granulated sugar

Coarsely ground white table sugar. Golden granulated sugar is unrefined and ideal for use in baking.

Caster sugar

A finely ground form of refined sugar used in baking because it is quick to dissolve. Golden caster sugar is unrefined and ideal for use in baking.

Icing sugar

This white sugar, pulverized and reduced to a powder to which a little starch is added, is ideal for decorating desserts.

Vanilla sugar

If you can't buy this ready-made you can make your own by cutting one or two vanilla pods into small lengths. Put them into a screw-topped jar with 450 g (1 lb) granulated sugar and leave for a week or so. Remove the vanilla pods before using the sugar.

Soft brown sugars

These are made up of small crystals and can be light or dark in colour. They are slightly more 'refined' than other brown sugars and are used in waffles, pancakes and certain biscuits. Add a little to plain yogurt or fromage frais – it tastes a lot nicer than ordinary sugar.

Coloured sugars

Today there are a large number of coloured sugars in different forms. Give yourself a treat and use them to decorate your cakes. The little blond heads will look adorable!

Demerara sugar

This natural cane sugar is highly perfumed and is therefore ideal for baking, particularly fruit cakes.

Nuts

This book includes dishes made with nuts and nut derivatives. It is advisable for readers with known allergic reactions to nuts and nut derivatives and those who may be potentially vulnerable to these allergies – such as pregnant and nursing mothers, invalids, the elderly, babies and children – to avoid dishes made with nuts and nut oils. It is also prudent to check the labels of pre-prepared ingredients for the possible inclusion of nut derivatives.

Eggs

Some recipes include raw eggs. It is not advisable to serve those dishes to very young children, pregnant women, elderly people or anyone weakened by serious illness. Be sure that the eggs are as fresh as possible. If in any doubt, consult your doctor.

buckwheat

maize

chestnut

demerara

soft brown

coloured

Sweet flan pastry

Preparation time: 10 minutes
Cooking time: 15 minutes
You can prepare this the day before.

250 g (9 oz) flour
125 g (4½ oz) cold butter, cubed
100 g (4 oz) icing sugar
2 egg yolks
1 tablespoon milk
1 pinch of salt

Sieve the flour onto your work surface.
Make a well in the flour and put the butter and icing sugar into the hollow.
Rub together using your fingertips, then add the egg yolks, milk and pinch of salt.
Knead the pastry until it has a sandy consistency.
Then roll the pastry into a ball, wrap it in clingfilm and put it in the refrigerator for 2 hours.

TIP • You can flavour the pastry by adding the grated peel of a quarter of an unwaxed lemon or orange.

Sweet flan pastry with almonds

Preparation time: 10 minutes
Cooking time: 15 minutes

250 g (9 oz) flour
125 g (4½ oz) cold butter, cubed
100 g (4 oz) ground almonds
2 egg yolks
1 tablespoon milk
1 pinch of salt

Sieve the flour onto your work surface.
Make a well in the flour and put the butter and ground almonds into the hollow.
Rub together using your fingertips, then add the egg yolks, milk and salt.
Knead the pastry until it has a sandy consistency.
Then roll the pastry into a ball, wrap it in clingfilm and put it in the refrigerator for 2 hours.

TIP • If you haven't got a rolling pin, you can make mini-tartlets by putting a ball of pastry in the freezer for 30 minutes and then cutting it into slices 3–4 mm (about ⅛ inch) thick.

Here are three classic pastry recipes that are quick and easy, and fun to make. They occur frequently in this book.

Shortcrust pastry

Preparation time: 10 minutes
Cooking time: 15 minutes
You can prepare this the day before.

250 g (9 oz) flour
1 pinch of salt
50 ml (2 fl oz) water
125 g (4½ oz) butter (at room temperature), cubed
1 egg yolk
40 g (1½ oz) caster sugar

Sieve the flour onto your work surface.
Pour the salt into the water to dissolve it.
Make a well in the flour and put the butter into the hollow. Rub together using your fingertips until the mixture resembles fine breadcrumbs.
Roll the pastry into a ball and then make another well. Put the egg yolk, sugar, salt and water in the hollow. Knead the pastry as quickly as possibly, then roll it into a ball, wrap it in clingfilm and put it in the refrigerator for about 1 hour.

TIP • Do not knead your pastry for too long. Shortcrust pastry can be used for both sweet and savoury recipes. For the latter, omit the sugar.

Shortcrust pastry

Bitter orange marmalade
Preparation time: 15 minutes
Cooking time: 50 minutes

1 copper or stainless steel preserving pan
about 6 500 g (1 lb) jars

12 to 15 unwaxed bitter oranges
1 lemon
1 kg (2¼ lb) granulated sugar

First sterilize the jars (see TIP below).
Remove the rind from 3 of the oranges. Cut it
into thin strips. Heat some water in a small
saucepan. As soon as it boils drop in the rind and
poach for 2 to 3 minutes, then remove the rind
and drain.
Squeeze the oranges and put the juice and flesh
in the preserving pan.
Squeeze the lemon and add the juice to the pan.
Add the sugar, stir once and cook the mixture
over a moderate heat for about 30 minutes.
Next add the strained peel and continue to cook
for another 20 minutes.
Allow to cool a little before transferring to jars.
Seal the jars.
When they are cold, store them in a cool, dry
place away from light.

Strawberry jam
Preparation time: 30 minutes
Cooking time: 20 minutes

1 copper or stainless steel preserving pan
3–4 500 g (1 lb) jars

1.2 kg (2 lb 12 oz) strawberries
850 g (1¾ lb) granulated sugar
juice of 1 lemon

First sterilize the jars (see TIP below).
Quickly wash the strawberries under cold running
water, remove the hulls and drain the fruit. Put
them in a bowl with the sugar and lemon juice.
Cover with clingfilm and leave in a cold place
overnight.
The next day remove the strawberries from the
bowl with a skimmer and keep to one side. Pour
the juice into the preserving pan and boil rapidly
for 10 to 12 minutes. Regularly skim off the
foam that forms on the surface. Pour in the
strawberries and cook for about 10 minutes.
Then skim.
Put the jam into the jars immediately, close and
seal them.
When they are cold, store them in a cool, dry
place away from light.

TIP • Before using preserving jars, you should
wash and dry them. Then place in a pan of
boiling water for several minutes in order to
sterilize them. Stand the jars upside down to
drain on a clean tea towel. You may also
sterilize them in your oven at 110°C (225°F), Gas
Mark ¼ for 5 minutes.

Cherries in syrup
Sufficient to fill a 1 litre (1¾ pint) jar
Preparation time: 30 minutes
Cooking time: 20 minutes

1 1 litre, (1¾ pint) glass jar

600 g (1 lb 5 oz) cherries
2 tablespoons caster sugar
1 heaped teaspoon vanilla sugar

Quickly wash the cherries under cold running
water, drain them and remove the stalks.
Fill the jar with cherries, then pour in cold, boiled
water until it reaches halfway up the jar.
Add the caster sugar and the vanilla sugar.
Seal the jar and sterilize it for 20 minutes in a pan
of boiling water. The jar must be completely
submerged. Leave to cool in the pan.
Store the jar in a cool, dry place away from light.
Your cherries in syrup can be kept like this for up
to a year.

Apricots in syrup
Sufficient to fill a 1 litre (1¾ pint) jar
Preparation time: 30 minutes
Cooking time: 20 minutes

1 1 litre (1¾ pint) glass jar

850 g (1 lb 14 oz) apricots
2 tablespoons icing sugar
1 heaped teaspoon vanilla sugar

Wash the apricots and drain. Cut them in half and
remove the stones. Break 4 or 5 stones and place
the kernels in the jar. Fill it up with the apricots.
Pour in cold boiled water until it reaches halfway
up the jar. Add the icing sugar and the vanilla
sugar.
Seal the jar and sterilize it for 20 minutes in a pan
of boiling water. The jar must be completely
submerged. Leave to cool in the pan.
Store the jar in a cool, dry place away from light.
Your apricots in syrup can be kept like this for up
to a year.

Custard

Serves 4–6
Preparation time: 5 minutes
Cooking time: 5 minutes

1 vanilla pod
1 litre (1¾ pints) milk
8 egg yolks
200 g (7 oz) caster sugar

Split the vanilla pod in two lengthways and score it well. Pour the milk into a large heavy-based saucepan, add the vanilla pod and heat to simmering point.
Beat the egg yolks and the sugar in a large bowl until the mixture becomes slightly frothy and takes on a pretty cream colour.
Remove the vanilla pod from the saucepan and slowly pour the warm milk onto the egg-sugar mixture, stirring all the time.
Pour the custard back into the saucepan and cook on a low heat while continuing to stir. The custard is cooked when it thickens and coats the spoon. Remove the pan from the heat and leave to cool.
Custard (also known as crème anglaise) is easy to make but it must not be allowed to boil. If any lumps occur, you can use an electric mixer to dissolve them.

Crème brûlée

The well-known crème brûlée (literally 'burnt cream') is made from the same ingredients as custard. However, you only use 300 ml (10 fl oz) of milk and make up the difference with 700 ml (1¼ pints) double cream.
Beat the egg yolks and sugar together, warm the milk and cream and pour them into the mixture, stirring all the time. Divide the mixture into individual ramekin dishes and bake in a bain-marie (stand the dishes in a baking tin containing boiling water) in the oven for about 20 minutes at 150°C (300°F) Gas Mark 2.
Just before serving, dust the dishes with demerara sugar or soft brown sugar and put them in a gratin dish surrounded by ice cubes. Heat the grill to maximum and place the ramekins and the gratin dish just under the heat. Don't take your eye off it!
Serve as soon as the sugar has caramelized.

Baked custard

Use exactly the same ingredients as for custard. Beat the egg yolks and sugar until the mixture becomes slightly frothy and takes on a pretty cream colour. Pour the mixture onto the warm milk, stirring all the time.
Divide the custard into individual ramekin dishes and bake in a bain-marie (stand the dishes in a shallow baking tin containing boiling water) in the oven for about 20 minutes at 150°C (300°F) Gas Mark 2.

Confectioner's custard (Crème pâtissière)

Serves 4–6
Preparation time: 5 minutes
Cooking time: 8 minutes

250 ml (9 fl oz) milk
½ vanilla pod split in two lengthways
2 egg yolks
3 tablespoons caster sugar
2 tablespoons cornflour

Pour the milk into a heavy-based pan, add the vanilla and heat to simmering point.
Mix the egg yolks and sugar in a large bowl then add the cornflour, stirring all the time.
Slowly pour in the warm milk and mix.
Pour the mixture into a pan and let it thicken over a low heat, stirring constantly with a wooden spoon.
Leave the crème pâtissière to cool before using it to enhance your cakes.
If you like you can flavour your crème pâtissière with a few drops of rum or Grand Marnier.

BUTTER is, needless to say, an essential ingredient for successful home baking. Here are a few tips on how to use it.

Salted butter

You can always find salted butter in the dairy section of your supermarket. It will lend a subtle taste to all your sweet recipes. It's up to you whether you choose salted or unsalted butter, according to your taste. Certain desserts are more suited to one or the other. For example, an upside-down cake (tarte Tatin) made with salted butter is exquisite.

Use in cakes and pastries

Take your butter out of the refrigerator half an hour or an hour before you start cooking, cut it into small cubes and leave it to reach room temperature. It will then be easy to use.

Butter cream

Butter cream is ideal for filling a Swiss roll (page 134) or a sponge cake (page 64).

Sufficient for 1 cake
Preparation time: 15 minutes
Cooking time: 5 minutes

100 g (4 oz) sugar
100 ml (4 fl oz) water
250 g (9 oz) butter
5 egg yolks

Dissolve the sugar in the water to make a clear syrup.
Cream the butter to soften it, pour the syrup onto the butter and whisk together.
Add the egg yolks, one at a time.
Flavour with vanilla, coffee or chocolate (a few drops of vanilla extract or coffee essence will be sufficient, or 1 or 2 tablespoons of cocoa powder).

TIP • For a 'lighter' butter cream, whisk 3 egg whites with the sugar syrup and add to the softened butter. Don't forget the egg yolks!

Crème Chantilly

Like sweet flan pastry, homemade crème Chantilly is out of this world!

You can adjust the quantity of cream each time you make it, according to how much you need.

300 ml (½ pint) double cream
1 heaped teaspoon vanilla sugar

The cream must be very cold so put it in the bowl in which it will be whisked and place in the coldest part of the refrigerator. Leave it there for half an hour at least.
Remove the bowl from the refrigerator and pour in the vanilla sugar.
Use an electric whisk. If yours has several speeds, increase the speed gradually. The cream will become frothy and then thicken slightly. As soon as the cream sticks to the beaters it is ready! It is important to stop at the right time, otherwise it will turn to butter.

TIP • Home-made crème Chantilly does not keep well. It should be eaten the same day or it may go off.
Use double rather than whipping cream as it will thicken more easily.

Red fruit coulis

You may be able to buy ready-made frozen coulis but it is not difficult to make.
You can use all sorts of red fruit: raspberries, blackcurrants, redcurrants etc.
If you see red fruit in the market that are slightly past their best, you should buy them as they are ideal for making coulis. After washing the fruit, blend them in a food processor with caster sugar to taste. Strain to remove the pips.
You can easily freeze your coulis and use it when you need to.

TIP • Store it in an ice-tray as ice cubes; that way you need only thaw the right quantity.

Tea and coffee breaks

Chocolate madeleines

For a tasty alternative, replace 100 g (4 oz) flour with 150 g (5 oz) good quality dark chocolate. Leave out the orange flower water.

Honey madeleines

If you have access to some good honey from a beekeeper, you should try this. Simply replace 150 g (5 oz) sugar with 150 g (5 oz) honey. If your honey has solidified let it melt with the butter for a few minutes. Leave out the orange flower water.

Madeleines

Serves 4–6
Preparation time: 15 minutes
Cooking time: 10 minutes

1 bun tray

5 eggs
1 pinch of salt
150 g (5 oz) salted butter + 20 g (¾ oz) for greasing the bun tray
200 g (7 oz) caster sugar
8 drops of flowers of orange water
200 g (7 oz) plain flour

Preheat the oven to 180°C (350°F) Gas Mark 4.
Grease the bun tray with butter.
Break the eggs and separate the whites from the yolks.
Add a pinch of salt to the whites and, using a whisk, beat them until stiff.
Melt the butter gently in a small heavy-based saucepan.
Whisk the egg yolks with the sugar and then add the melted butter and the orange flower water.
Gradually add the beaten egg whites and the flour.
Fill each hollow of the bun tray using a spoon.
Place the tray in the oven and cook for about 10 minutes.
Then take it out of the oven and ease the madeleines from the tray.
The madeleines can be eaten while still warm but can also be kept for a few days in an airtight tin.

Coconut rock cakes

Serves 4
Preparation time: 15 minutes
Cooking time: 5 minutes

1 baking sheet lined with nonstick baking paper

180 g (6 oz) grated coconut
120 g (4½ oz) caster sugar
2 fresh egg whites
½ teaspoon vanilla extract

Preheat the oven to 210°C (410°F) Gas Mark 6–7.
Using your fingertips, mix together the coconut,
sugar, egg white and vanilla extract in a bowl.
Roll into little balls of equal size in your hands and
place them on the baking sheet (if you like you
can give them a pyramid shape like the ones you
see in bakers' shops).
Leave sufficient space between the balls to
prevent them sticking together during cooking.
Put them in the oven for 5 minutes – no longer –
then take them out and leave to cool at room
temperature.

Almond brittle

Serves 4–6
Preparation time: 10 minutes
Cooking time: 40 minutes

1 sandwich tin or baking sheet

2 whole eggs + 1 yolk
250 g (9 oz) caster sugar
2 tablespoons brandy
1 pinch of salt
250 g (9 oz) salted butter (at room
temperature), cubed + 20 g (¾ oz) for greasing
the tin
450 g (1 lb) plain flour
100 g (4 oz) almonds
3 tablespoons milk

Preheat the oven to 180°C (350°F) Gas Mark 4.
Grease the tin with the butter.
Mix the 2 eggs with the sugar, brandy and salt in
a large bowl.
Add the butter (at room temperature) and mix
well.
Pour in the flour in a stream, stirring all the time.
Add the almonds.
Do not work the mixture too much and use only
the fingertips.
Spread the mixture in the tin, smoothing the
surface with a spatula. Make a criss-cross pattern
with the prongs of a fork. Mix the milk and the
egg yolk in a bowl and use this to glaze the
mixture.
Bake in the oven for 35 to 40 minutes.
Leave the brittle to cool before removing it from
the tin.

Hearth cake
(Galette Saint-Pierre)

It's best if you use your hands for this recipe! It's not worth getting out your food processor. You won't even need a wooden spoon. (Re)discover the pleasure of kneading with your hands.

Serves 6
Preparation time: 15 minutes
Cooking time: 25 minutes

1 sandwich tin or a number of small tins

250 g (9 oz) plain flour
1 teaspoon baking powder
5 egg yolks + 1 egg yolk for glazing
150 g (5 oz) caster sugar
1 pinch of salt (if you're using unsalted butter)
180 g (6 oz) salted butter (at room temperature), cubed + 10 g (½ oz) for greasing the tin

Preheat the oven to 180°C (350°F) Gas Mark 4. Lightly grease the tin.
Mix the flour and the baking powder then sift onto a work surface or into a basin.
Make a well in the centre and put in it the 5 egg yolks, sugar and salt. Mix well with the fingertips until the mixture takes on a sandy consistency. Then add the cubed butter to the pastry and mix again.
Put the mixture into the tin(s). Using a brush, glaze the surface with a little beaten egg yolk. Make a criss-cross pattern with the prongs of a fork.
Put the cake in the oven for about 25 minutes. Remove it from the tin while still warm and leave to cool on a cake rack.

Meringues

Serves 4
Preparation time: 15 minutes
Cooking time: 55 minutes

1 baking sheet lined with nonstick baking paper

2 eggs
1 small pinch of salt
2 heaped teaspoons vanilla sugar
60 g (2½ oz) caster sugar
70 g (3 oz) icing sugar

Preheat the over to 150°C (300°F) Gas Mark 2.
Break the eggs and separate the whites from the yolks.
Add the salt to the egg whites and beat them with your electric whisk until they form stiff peaks.
Gradually add the vanilla sugar, beating all the time. Then gradually pour in the caster sugar and icing sugar while continuing to beat.
Using 2 teaspoons, divide the mixture into small blobs all the same size and each with a pointed tip.
Line them out on the baking sheet as you go, leaving a 2 to 3 cm (1 inch) space between them.
Place the baking sheet in the oven and immediately lower the temperature to 140°C (275°F), Gas Mark 1.
Leave to cook slowly for 55 minutes, then gently open the oven door for a few minutes. Close the door and turn off the oven. Leave the meringues inside the oven for another hour. This will make them crunchy. You can keep them for several days in a biscuit tin.

Almond squares

Serves 6
Preparation time: 20 minutes
Cooking time: 8 minutes

1 baking sheet

2 egg whites
50 g (2 oz) icing sugar
30 g (1 oz) plain flour + 10 g (½ oz) to dust the
baking sheet
30 g (1 oz) salted butter, melted + 20 g (¾ oz)
to grease the baking sheet
60 g (2 oz) almonds, chopped or slivered

Preheat the oven to 210° (410°F) Gas Mark 6–7.
Grease the baking sheet with butter and dust
lightly with flour.
Whisk the egg whites and icing sugar to form a
light frothy mixture. Add the flour and the melted
butter, stirring all the time with a spatula.
Then place small heaps of the mixture on the
sheet, approximately 3 cm (1¼ inches) apart.
Flatten the heaps with the blade of a knife and
sprinkle with the almonds.
Put in the oven for about 8 minutes.
Roll up the squares while still warm, as soon as
they come out of the oven, by wrapping them
round a mini rolling pin (or wooden spoon
handle).

Cats' tongues (Langues de chat)

Serves 4
Preparation time: 20 minutes
Cooking time: 6 minutes

1 baking sheet

50 g (2 oz) butter (at room temperature), cubed
+ 20 g (¾ oz) for greasing the baking sheet
50 g (2 oz) icing sugar
1 egg white
60 g (2½ oz) plain flour

Preheat the oven to 180°C (350°F) Gas Mark 4.
Grease the baking sheet with butter.
Cream together the butter and sugar to an oily consistency.
Whisk the egg white to form stiff peaks and fold them gently into the butter-sugar mixture, then pour in the flour in a stream, stirring all the time.
Line out the cats' tongues on the baking sheet leaving a 3 cm (1½ inch) gap between each one so that they don't touch during the cooking process. You can do this with a piping bag and a 6-mm (¼-inch) diameter nozzle or shape them using two teaspoons.
Place in the oven for about 6 minutes. Keep a close eye on the cooking. They should be a pretty blond colour and slightly brown at the edges. Allow to cool before trying them.
You can easily keep them for several days in a biscuit tin.

Chocolate cookies

Serves 4–6
Preparation time: 15 minutes
Cooking time: 10 minutes

1 baking sheet lined with nonstick baking paper

100 g (4 oz) salted butter
200 g (7 oz) dark chocolate (at least 70% cocoa solids)
80 g (3 oz) caster sugar
100 g (4 oz) plain flour
1 teaspoon baking powder
1 egg
50 g (2 oz) ground almonds

Preheat the oven to 200°C (400°F) Gas Mark 6.
Slowly melt the butter in a small heavy-based pan then remove from the heat.
Grate the chocolate. Blend the melted butter and sugar to make a frothy mixture.
Mix the flour and baking powder in a bowl. Pour them into the butter-sugar mixture, together with the egg, ground almonds and chocolate. Mix thoroughly.
Place the mixture in small rounds on the baking sheet, leaving a space between each one. Cook in the oven for 10 minutes.
Leave to cool before trying them.

New York brownies

Serves 4–6
Preparation time: 15 minutes
Cooking time: 25 minutes

1 square tin

200 g (7 oz) dark chocolate (at least 70% cocoa solids)
120 g (4½ oz) salted butter, at room temperature, cubed + 20 g (¾ oz) for greasing the tin
160 g (5 oz) caster sugar
3 eggs
70 g (2½ oz) plain flour + 10 g (½ oz) for dusting the tin
100 g (4 oz) hazelnuts or almonds, roughly chopped (optional)

Preheat the oven to 150°C (300°F) Gas Mark 2.
Grease the tin with butter and lightly dust with flour.
Break the chocolate into pieces. Melt in a pan over boiling water or in a microwave oven.
In another bowl work the butter and sugar together with a spatula to form a smooth paste.
Add the eggs one by one, stirring all the time, then pour in the flour in a stream, still stirring.
Pour in the melted chocolate and the hazelnuts and mix well. Spread the mixture in the tin and cook in the oven for about 25 minutes.
Allow to cool before cutting into squares.

Muffins

Serves 4–6
Preparation time: 10 minutes
Cooking time: 20 minutes

12 muffin tins

125 g (4½ oz) salted butter + 20 g (¾ oz) for greasing the tins
300 g (10½ oz) plain flour
½ teaspoon baking powder
1 teaspoon ground ginger
120 g (4½ oz) golden caster sugar
100 g (4 oz) chopped almonds
2 eggs
200 ml (7 fl oz) milk

Preheat the oven to 200°C (400°F) Gas Mark 6.
Thoroughly grease the tins with butter.
Slowly melt the butter in a heavy-based saucepan.
Mix the flour, baking powder and ginger in a bowl and then add the sugar and almonds.
Whisk the eggs and the milk in a large bowl. Add the melted butter and mix.
Fill three-quarters of each tin with the mixture.
Put in the oven for about 20 minutes.
Allow to cool for 5 minutes before removing the muffins from the tins.

VARIATION • You can replace the chopped almonds with sultanas, chocolate drops, blackcurrants or blueberries.

Chocolate truffles

Serves 4
Preparation time: 10 minutes
Cooking time: 5 minutes

100 g (4 oz) dark chocolate (at least 70% cocoa
solids)
50 g (2 oz) caster sugar
2 tablespoons milk
50 g (2 oz) butter
1 fresh egg
4 tablespoons cocoa powder

Break the chocolate into small pieces and place
them in a large heavy-based saucepan with the
sugar, milk and butter.
Gently melt the mixture over a low heat, stirring
all the time until it is completely smooth. Remove
the pan from the heat.
Break the egg and separate the yolk from the
white.
Pour the yolk into the chocolate cream and blend
rapidly.
Leave the mixture to cool then place in the
refrigerator for about 1 hour while it sets. Then
shape the truffles: pour some cocoa powder into
a plate; take a ball of paste and roll it quickly in
the palm of your hand; then roll it in the cocoa
powder.
Put the truffles in the refrigerator for at least
1 hour and serve while still cold.

TIP • If you like, you can flavour these truffles
with alcohol: Grand Marnier, rum or brandy for
instance.
Eat them quickly (it will not be difficult!) as they
are delicate and cannot be kept for long.

Christmas biscuits

Makes about 1 kg (2 lb 4 oz) biscuits
Preparation time: 20 minutes
Cooking time: 10–12 minutes per batch
Start the day before you want to cook them.

pastry cutters
1 baking sheet

250 g (9 oz) butter (at room temperature),
cubed + 20 g (¾ oz) for greasing the baking
sheet
200 g (7 oz) caster sugar
400 g (14 oz) plain flour
150 g (5 oz) ground almonds
2 whole eggs + 3 yolks
2 heaped teaspoons vanilla sugar (see page 12)
2 teaspoons ground cinnamon

Beat together the butter and sugar until the
mixture turns slightly pale. Add the flour and the
ground almonds, then the 2 whole eggs, beating
all the time. Pour in the vanilla sugar and the
ground cinnamon and stir.
Make the pastry into a ball, wrap it in clingfilm
and put it in the refrigerator for at least 3 hours.
Ideally you should prepare it the day before and
leave it to chill overnight.
Preheat the oven to 180°C (350°F) Gas Mark 4.
Grease the baking sheet with the butter.
Take the pastry out of the refrigerator just before
you want to use it. Roll it out to a thickness of
about 4 mm (⅛ inch), cut out the biscuits with the
pastry cutters and arrange them on the baking
sheet. Brush the tops with a little beaten egg yolk
and cook in the oven for 10–12 minutes.
Watch them carefully. When done, the biscuits
should be a golden colour.

Cinnamon and cider cakes

Serves 4–6
Preparation time: 15 minutes
Cooking time: 50 minutes

individual round tins, tartlet tins (or a loaf tin)

220 g (8 oz) plain flour
1 teaspoon baking powder
120 g (4½ oz) butter (at room temperature),
cubed + 20 g (¾ oz) for greasing the tin
120 g (4½ oz) caster sugar
2 eggs
1 teaspoon ground cinnamon
200 ml (7 fl oz) sweet cider

Preheat the oven to 180°C (350°F) Gas Mark 4.
Grease the tins with butter.
Combine the flour and baking powder in a bowl.
Blend the butter and sugar in another bowl until
the mixture becomes slightly frothy and light
yellow in colour, then add the eggs and half the
flour and cinnamon. Pour in the cider, a little at a
time, and the remainder of the flour in a stream.
Pour the mixture into the tins.
Put the tins in the oven for about 50 minutes.
Allow the cakes to cool for about 10 minutes
before removing them from the tins.

Breton biscuits

Serves 6
Preparation time: 15 minutes
Cooking time: 25 minutes

This is a variation of the Galette Saint-Pierre (see
page 32). Use the same quantities and the same
proportions. Divide your mixture into as many
small tins as you like. It really is delicious served
with bergamot tea or strong coffee.

Monks' tartlets with dark chocolate

Makes 6 tartlets
Preparation time: 15 minutes
Cooking time: 20 minutes

6 tartlet tins 10 cm (4 inches) in diameter

20 g (¾ oz) butter for greasing the tins
350 g (12 oz) shortcrust pastry
100 g (4 oz) dark chocolate (at least 70% cocoa
solids)
80 g (3 oz) ground almonds
60 g (2 oz) sultanas
60 g (2 oz) pine nuts

Preheat the oven to 180°C (350°F) Gas Mark 4.
Grease the tins with butter.
Roll out the shortcrust pastry and cut out 6 rounds
each approximately 14 cm (6 inches) in diameter.
Place one round of pastry in each tin, pressing
lightly into place with your fingers. Prick the bases
with a fork.
Break the chocolate into small pieces. Sprinkle the
ground almonds, the sultanas, the pine nuts and
the pieces of chocolate on the tart bases.
Now cut out 6 more rounds of pastry
approximately 10 cm (4 inches) in diameter. Place
them over the contents of the tartlets, making
sure that the edges are sealed.
Put in the oven for about 20 minutes.
Remove the tartlets from the tins immediately and
leave to cool. They are delicious eaten warm.

Traditional Norfolk cakes

Serves 4–6
Preparation time: 10 minutes
Cooking time: 50 minutes

individual round tins, tartlet tins (or a loaf tin)

200 g (7 oz) plain flour
1 teaspoon baking powder
120 g (4½ oz) salted butter, at room
temperature, cubed + 20 g (¾ oz) for greasing
the tin
120 g (4½ oz) caster sugar
200 g (7 oz) sultanas
1 tablespoon cider vinegar
150 ml (5 fl oz) milk

Preheat the oven to 180° (350°F) Gas Mark 4.
Grease the tins with butter.
Blend the flour and baking powder in a large
bowl. Add the butter and rub in with the
fingertips until it reaches a sandy consistency. Add
the sugar and the sultanas. Pour in the cider
vinegar and then the milk. Mix well.
Pour the mixture into the tins.
Cook in the oven for about 50 minutes
Check to see if they are done by piercing one of
the cakes with the blade of a knife. It should
come out clean. Leave to cool before taking the
cakes out of the tins.

Flutes

Makes 24 cakes
Preparation time: 15 minutes
Cooking time: 1¼ hours
Prepare the day before you want to eat them.

24 flute or muffin tins

20 g (¾ oz) butter for greasing the tins
1 whole egg + 4 yolks
1 litre (1¾ pints) milk
500 g (1 lb 2 oz) caster sugar
3 capfuls rum
5 drops vanilla extract
250 g (9 oz) plain flour

Blend the whole egg, yolks, milk, sugar, rum and vanilla extract in a large bowl.
Put the flour in a basin; make a well in the flour and add the mixture; mix well together, cover with clingfilm and leave for 24 hours in the refrigerator.
Heat the oven to 150°C (300°F) Gas Mark 2.
Grease the tins with butter.
Fill the tins two-thirds full with the mixture.
Cook for 1¼ hours. Remove the flutes from the tins and serve warm or cold.

Apple doughnuts

Serves 4–6
Preparation time: 20 minutes
Cooking time: 5 minutes

1 deep fryer

2 eggs
250 g (9 oz) plain flour
200 ml (7 fl oz) milk
50 ml (2 fl oz) beer
60 g (2½ oz) caster sugar
2 pinches of salt
4 apples
oil for frying
icing sugar

Break the eggs, separating the whites from the yolks.
Sift the flour, make a well and gradually beat in the milk a little at a time, together with the beer, the 2 egg yolks, the sugar and 1 pinch of salt.
When the mixture is smooth put it in the refrigerator and leave it for at least 30 minutes.
Peel the apples, remove the cores and the pips and cut into rounds about ½ cm (¼ inch) thick.
Add the other pinch of salt to the egg whites and, using a whisk, beat until they form stiff peaks; then gently fold in the mixture from the refrigerator.
Heat the oil in the deep fryer.
Dip each apple round into the batter and then immediately into the hot oil. When the doughnuts have turned golden all over use a slotted spoon to lift them out of the oil.
Drain the doughnuts on kitchen paper. Dust them with a little icing sugar just before serving.

Crunchy biscuits

Serves 4–6
Preparation time: 15 minutes
Cooking time: 8 minutes

different shaped pastry cutters
1 baking sheet

180 g (6 oz) plain flour
1 pinch of baking powder
120 g (4½ oz) salted butter (at room temperature), cubed + 20 g (¾ oz) for greasing the baking sheet
60 g (2 oz) caster sugar
1 egg
1 teaspoon vanilla extract
1 pinch of salt

Sift the flour and baking powder into a large bowl.
Tip the contents out onto your work surface and make a well in the flour. Fill the hollow with the butter and sugar and rub together with your fingertips until the mixture resembles fine breadcrumbs.
Make another well and pour in the egg and vanilla extract. Add the salt and mix well.
Roll the pastry into a ball, wrap it in clingfilm and put it in the refrigerator for 2 hours.
Preheat the oven to 180° (350°F) Gas Mark 4.
Grease the baking sheet.
Roll out the pastry on a floured surface.
Cut out biscuits with the pastry cutters and put them on the baking sheet.
Cook them in the oven for 6 to 8 minutes. The little biscuits should take on a golden hue. Watch them carefully.
Then take them out of the oven and leave to cool.
They will keep for a few days in an airtight tin.

Palmiers

Serves 4–6
Preparation time: 10 minutes
Cooking time: 10 minutes

1 baking sheet lined with nonstick baking paper
1 cake rack

1 roll of puff pastry
75 g (3 oz) caster sugar

Preheat the oven to 180°C (350°F) Gas Mark 4.
Roll out the pastry and dust with caster sugar, then roll each edge towards the middle. Place in the freezer for 5 minutes. Then cut it into thin strips and place them on the baking sheet.
Cook for about 10 minutes, taking care not to let them burn.
Leave to cool on a cake rack.

Almond and orange cake

Serves 6
Preparation time: 10 minutes
Cooking time: 40 minutes

1 loaf tin (or a number of small tins)

20 g (¾ oz) butter for greasing the tin
50 g (2 oz) plain flour
1 teaspoon baking powder
6 eggs
120 g (4½ oz) caster sugar
1 pinch of salt
240 g (9 oz) ground almonds
grated rind of 1 unwaxed orange
juice of 2 oranges

Preheat the oven to 180°C (350°F) Gas Mark 4.
Grease the tin with butter.
Mix together the flour and baking powder.
Break the eggs and separate the whites from the
yolks.
Whisk the yolks and sugar together until the
mixture turns slightly pale. Combine with the
flour and baking powder.
Add the pinch of salt to the egg whites and whisk
into firm peaks with your electric beater (or hand
whisk).
Then add the ground almonds to the first mixture,
pour in the orange rind and juice and fold in the
beaten egg whites a little at a time, using
sweeping movements so as not to break down
the egg whites. Fill the tin with this mixture and
put it in the oven for 40 minutes.
Decorate the cake when it has cooled with a little
icing sugar or coat it with vanilla icing.

Almond dainties

Serves 4–6
Preparation time: 20 minutes
Cooking time: 12 minutes

1 bun tray

70 g (2½ oz) salted butter + 20 g (¾ oz) for
greasing the tins
125 g (4½ oz) caster sugar
125 g (4½ oz) ground almonds
2 eggs
20 g (¾ oz) plain flour

Preheat the oven to 190°C (375°F) Gas Mark 5.
Grease the tray with butter.
Slowly melt the butter in a small heavy-based
saucepan.
Mix the sugar and ground almonds in a bowl
then gradually add the eggs.
Pour in the melted butter and mix well.
Finally, add the flour, stirring all the time.
Fill the tins with the mixture and cook in the oven
for about 12 minutes.

Some exotic variations
With ginger

For a slightly more spicy flavour add
2 tablespoons of chopped preserved ginger to
your mixture.

With green tea

Add 2 teaspoons of powdered green tea to the
ground almonds. (Green tea powder is available
at shops selling Chinese specialities.)

Almond dainties with green tea

Almond antlers

Serves 6–8
Preparation time: 30 minutes
Cooking time: 10–15 minutes

1 baking sheet
1 cake rack

500 g (1 lb 2 oz) ground almonds
150 g (5 oz) caster sugar
270 g (9½ oz) salted butter (at room
temperature) + 20 g (¾ oz) for greasing the
baking sheet
1 tablespoon water
500 g (1 lb 2 oz) plain flour + 10 g (½ oz) for
dusting the baking sheet
1 pinch of salt
3 tablespoons orange flower water
icing sugar

Almond pastry

Mix the ground almonds and sugar with 40 g
(1½ oz) butter. Add a tablespoon of water to
make a smooth paste. Knead it with your
fingertips then leave for about 30 minutes.

Biscuit mixture

Melt the rest of the butter in a small heavy-based
saucepan. Then mix it in a large bowl with the
flour, add the salt and stir well. The mixture
should be fairly firm.

Making the biscuits

Preheat the oven to 150°C (300°F) Gas Mark 2.
Grease the baking sheet and dust with flour.
Sprinkle flour on your work surface and roll out
the pastry thinly. Cut out small rectangles using a
pastry wheel.
Roll the almond paste into little sausage shapes
and place in the middle of each pastry rectangle.
Roll up the pastry into the shape of a horn.
Place the crescent shapes on the baking sheet.
Cook in the oven for about 10 minutes.
Keep an eye on the cooking as they must not be
allowed to brown.
Sprinkle lightly with orange flower water then roll
them gently in the icing sugar. Put them on a
cake rack and leave to cool.

Apple and cinnamon turnovers

Serves 4–6
Preparation time: 15 minutes
Cooking time: 40 minutes

1 baking sheet lined with nonstick baking paper

500 g (1 lb 2 oz) apples
2 tablespoons water
60 g (2½ oz) caster sugar
½ teaspoon ground cinnamon
400 g (14 oz) puff pastry
1 egg yolk

Peel and quarter the apples, remove the cores and pips. Put them in a pan with 2 tablespoons of water and the sugar.
Bring to the boil, turn down the heat. Leave to cook slowly for about 15 minutes. Dust with the ground cinnamon.
Preheat the oven to 180°C (350°F) Gas Mark 4.
Roll out the pastry and cut out rounds about 12 cm (4½ inches) in diameter.
Spread the apple compote over half of each round, leaving a space round the edge. Moisten the edges slightly and fold over the pastry to make the turnover. Glaze with a little beaten egg yolk and put in the oven. Cook for about 20–25 minutes.
Serve warm or cold.
You can decorate your turnovers with raw apple if you like.

Marvels

These little marvels used to be served on Shrove Tuesday in some countries but of course you can make them all the year round … and preferably with the help of children (they love making them!).

Preparation time: 15 minutes
Cooking time: 4 minutes

1 deep fryer

500 g (1 lb 2 oz) plain flour
2 teaspoons baking powder
100 g (4 oz) caster sugar
100 g (4 oz) salted butter (at room temperature), cubed
4 eggs
2 tablespoons rum
icing sugar

Mix the flour and baking powder then make a well. Put the sugar, cubed butter, eggs and rum into the hollow.
Mix with the fingertips then roll the dough into a ball and wrap in clingfilm. Put in the refrigerator for about 30 minutes.
Divide the dough into 3 or 4 balls then roll out each one on a lightly floured surface.
Cut out small rectangles of dough about 4 cm (1½ inches) wide. Make a slit in the middle and fold back a flap of dough to resemble a bow.
Heat the oil in a fryer. Drop in a bit of pastry – it if rises to the surface the oil is at the right temperature.
Cook the marvels by plunging them into the cooking oil. Watch them carefully as the marvels need to be just right: golden but not burnt.
Drain on kitchen paper. Dust with icing sugar and serve immediately.
They can also be kept for several days in a biscuit tin.

Apple and cinnamon turnovers

Choux pastry puffs

The great thing about choux pastry is that everyone is impressed by it ... even the cook! Yet nothing could be easier. Have a go!

Serves 4
Preparation time: 15 minutes
Cooking time: 25 minutes

1 baking sheet lined with nonstick baking paper

50 g (2 oz) butter
200 ml (7 fl oz) water
75 g (3 oz) plain flour
2 eggs
1 pinch of salt
30 g (1 oz) candy sugar (as illustrated)

Preheat the over to 150–180°C (300–350°F) Gas Mark 2–4.
Put the butter and water in a small heavy-based saucepan to heat. As soon as the first bubbles form, remove the pan from the heat.
Pour in the flour all at once and mix with a spoon until the mixture turns into a rubbery ball that detaches easily from the sides of the pan.
Add the eggs one at a time, stirring constantly, then add the salt. Your mixture should have a smooth but firm consistency.
Use 2 spoons to form small balls and arrange them on the baking sheet.
Warning! Leave a generous space between the puffs as they rise during cooking.
Put in the oven for about 15 minutes.
Remove from the oven and dust with candy sugar.

Milk rolls

Serves 4–6
Preparation time: 25 minutes
Cooking time: 12 minutes

1 baking sheet lined with nonstick baking paper

10 g (½ oz) dried yeast
50 ml (2 fl oz) + 50 ml (2 fl oz) milk
250 g (9 oz) plain flour
30 g (1 oz) caster sugar
1 pinch of salt
1 whole egg + 1 yolk
60 g (2½ oz) salted butter (at room temperature), cubed

Dissolve the yeast in 50 ml (2 fl oz) warm milk (or follow instructions on the packet).
Pour the flour, sugar, salt, the milk-yeast mixture and the whole egg into the bowl of your food processor. Blend, then pour in the rest of the milk and blend some more.
Knead the dough a little until smooth. Add the cubed butter and knead again.
Then form the dough into a ball and put it in a warm place covered with a tea towel. Leave for about 45 minutes, by which time it should have doubled in volume.
Preheat the oven to 210°C (410°F) Gas Mark 6–7. Glaze the buns with a little beaten egg yolk and put in the oven. Lower the temperature to 180°C (350°F), Gas Mark 4 and cook for about 12 minutes. Be vigilant during the cooking process. The rolls will be slightly brown underneath when done.
Using the same dough recipe you can make different shapes: plaits, coils, etc.

Choux pastry puffs

Currant buns

It is very satisfying to make your own bread. Depending on your mood, you can use chopped hazelnuts or walnuts instead of currants.

Serves 4–6
Preparation time: 20 minutes
Cooking time: 15 minutes

1 baking sheet lined with nonstick baking paper

1 sachet dried yeast
150 ml (5 fl oz) water
350 g (10½ oz) white plain flour
100 g (4 oz) wholemeal flour
10 g (½ oz) salted butter (at room temperature), cubed
10 g (½ oz) caster sugar
10 g (½ oz) salt
250 g (9 oz) currants or sultanas

Dissolve the yeast in 50 ml (2 fl oz) warm water (or follow directions on the packet).
Put the white flour, wholemeal flour, butter, caster sugar, salt and yeast in the bowl.
Using a food processor with a dough attachment if available, mix on a slow speed then pour in the remaining water, a little at a time. (Alternatively you can mix by hand using a spoon.)
Knead by hand for a few seconds until the dough forms a ball.
Put the dough in a warm place and cover with a tea towel. Leave it until it doubles in volume.
Add the currants or sultanas, knead again for a few seconds and then form dough into small balls and arrange them on the baking sheet. Cover with a tea towel and leave to rise again for about 45 minutes.
Preheat the oven to 210°C (410°F) Gas Mark 6–7. Brush the buns with a little water and bake them for about 15 minutes.
Check to see if they are done by tapping the bases of the buns. If they sound hollow, they are cooked!

Delicious
easy-to-make
cakes

Delicious easy-to-make cakes

Yogurt cake with jam

Yogurt cake

Without doubt yogurt cake has many outstanding advantages: it is very easy to make and always turns out well; it is also infinitely versatile. Use the empty yogurt pot to measure the ingredients. Here are a few examples. You can also invent your own.

Serves 4–6
Preparation time: 15 minutes
Cooking time: 35 minutes

1 deep sandwich tin 22 cm (9 inches) in diameter

15 g (½ oz) butter for greasing the tin
1 small pot of natural yogurt
2 pots of sugar
3 eggs
3 pots of plain flour
2 teaspoons baking powder
1 pot of cooking oil

Preheat the oven to 180°C (350°F) Gas Mark 4. Grease the tin with butter.
Pour the yogurt into a basin then rinse out the pot and use it to measure the other ingredients. Combine the yogurt, sugar and eggs; mix until frothy. Add the flour and baking powder; mix again then add the oil.
Put the mixture into the tin. Cook for about 35 minutes. Remove from the tin while still warm.

Simple variations

Replace the pot of oil with the same weight in butter.
Replace the pot of oil with double cream (the cake will be paler).
Substitute 1 pot of ground almonds for 1 pot of flour.

Pineapple upside-down cake

yogurt cake mixture (see above)
1 small can of pineapple slices in syrup
1 vanilla pod
1 tablespoon rum
rind of 1 lemon

For the caramel:
20 g (¾ oz) salted butter
3 tablespoons demerara or soft brown sugar
1 tablespoon pineapple syrup

First caramelize the pineapple: chop up 3 slices of the pineapple and leave to cook in a saucepan with the vanilla pod for about 10 minutes over a low heat.
Grease the tin well and arrange slices of pineapple over the base. Caramelize the butter, sugar and 1 tablespoon of pineapple juice in a saucepan: heat slowly while the sugar dissolves, then turn up the heat and watch carefully. When the mixture has caramelized slightly pour it over the pineapple in the base of the tin.

Prepare the yogurt cake mixture following the basic recipe and then add the rum, the lemon rind and the chopped, cooked pineapple.
Cover the pineapple slices with the mixture and cook in the oven for about 40 minutes at 180°C (350°F) Gas Mark 4.
When cooked, take the cake out of the oven and leave to stand for about 15 minutes before removing from the tin.

Lemon cake

yogurt cake mixture (see above)
juice of 2 lemons
½ pot of icing sugar
rind of 1 lemon

Follow the basic recipe, adding the lemon rind at the end. Bake in the oven for about 40 minutes at 180°C (350°F) Gas Mark 4.
When the cake is cooked, take it out of the oven and allow to cool before removing it from the tin. Make the lemon glaze by mixing the lemon juice and icing sugar. Brush over the cake, adding a little lemon peel for decoration.

Rum baba cake

yogurt cake mixture made with ground almonds (see under 'Simple variations' above)
350 ml (12 fl oz) rum
350 ml (12 fl oz) water
35 g (1½ oz) demerara sugar

Follow the basic recipe. Cook for about 40 minutes at 180°C (350°F) Gas Mark 4.
While the cake is cooking, boil the rum, water and sugar together over a low heat to make syrup. Remove the cake from the oven when cooked and douse with the syrup repeatedly until the baba is completely saturated. Leave to cool. Gently remove from the tin.

VARIATION • You can replace the rum with cherry juice mixed with kirsch but leave out the sugar. Arrange about 20 cherries in the tin before pouring in the cake mixture.

Apple cake

yogurt cake mixture made with double cream (see under 'Simple variations' above)
3 or 4 good quality apples, slightly acidic (e.g. Granny Smiths), chopped
rind of 1 lemon

Follow the basic recipe. At the end add the chopped apples and the lemon rind.
Put in the oven for 40 minutes at 180°C (350°F) Gas Mark 4.
When the cake is cooked, take it out of the oven and wait about 15 minutes before removing it from the tin.

Savoy sponge cake

Serves 4–6
Preparation time: 15 minutes
Cooking time: 35 minutes

1 deep sandwich tin 22 cm (about 9 inches) in diameter

20 g (¾ oz) butter for greasing the tin
10 g (½ oz) plain flour for dusting the tin
4 eggs
125 g (4½ oz) caster sugar
65 g (2½ oz) cornflour
1 pinch of salt

Preheat the oven to 150°C (300°F) Gas Mark 2.
Thoroughly grease the tin with butter and dust with flour.
Separate the egg yolks from the whites. Using an electric mixer if you wish, whisk together the yolks and sugar until frothy. Gradually add the cornflour. Mix well.
Add the salt to the egg whites and beat until stiff white peaks are formed then gently fold into the yolks-sugar mixture using a spatula so as not to deflate the egg whites. The mixture should be quite smooth.
Pour the mixture into the tin.
Put in the oven and bake for about 35 minutes.

Genoese sponge cake

You can also use this recipe to make a chocolate Genoese sponge. All you do is replace 30 g (1 oz) flour with 30 g (1 oz) cocoa powder.

Serves 4–6
Preparation time: 10 minutes
Cooking time: 25 minutes

1 deep sandwich tin 22 cm (about 9 inches) in diameter
1 cake rack

20 g (¾ oz) butter for greasing the tin
125 g (4½ oz) caster sugar
4 eggs
125 g (4½ oz) plain flour + 10 g (½ oz) for dusting the tin

Preheat the oven to 150°C (300°F) Gas Mark 2.
Grease the tin and dust lightly with flour.
Put the sugar and eggs in a large bowl.
Heat a large pan of water. When it reaches simmering point, place the bowl in the water. Whisk until the mixture thickens then remove the bowl from the water and continue to beat for a few more seconds.
Add the flour a little at a time, still mixing and lifting the mixture with a spatula.
Spread the mixture in the tin. Smooth the surface with a spatula.
Cook for about 25 minutes. The cake is ready when it is a lovely golden colour.
As soon as it is done remove the sponge from the tin and leave to cool on a cake rack.

Chocolate sandwich cake

Serves 4–6
Preparation time: 30 minutes
Cooking time: 40 minutes

1 Savoy sponge cake (see page 64)
200 g (7 oz) dark chocolate
2 tablespoons double cream
4 eggs

Soften the chocolate in boiling water for 20 minutes then pour off the hot water, leaving the chocolate. Immediately add the cream and mix well.
Separate the egg whites from the yolks.
Fold the yolks into chocolate one at a time. Beat the egg whites on a medium speed (or use a hand whisk) to form stiff peaks, adding a pinch of sugar half way through; then increase the speed.
Fold the beaten egg whites into the chocolate mixture. Refrigerate for a few hours.
Meanwhile make a Savoy sponge cake in a 22 cm (9 inch) diameter tin. When cooked remove immediately from the tin. Leave to cool, then cut in two horizontally.
Fill with the chocolate cream. Replace the top and keep in a cool place.

Mocha sandwich cake

Serves 4–6
Preparation time: 30 minutes
Cooking time: 40 minutes

1 Savoy sponge (see page 64)
butter cream (see page 20)
coffee essence

Make a Savoy sponge cake. Take it out of the tin as soon as it is done and leave to cool.
Cut it in two horizontally.
Fill with butter cream mixed with coffee essence. Replace the top. Coat the whole cake in butter cream and keep in a cool place.

Chestnut sandwich cake

Serves 4–6
Preparation time: 30 minutes
Cooking time: 40 minutes

1 Savoy sponge cake (see page 64)
3 large meringues
225 g (8 oz) chestnut spread

If you are unable to buy ready-made chestnut spread, you can make your own (see page 152).
Crumble the meringues.
Whip the chestnut spread and combine with the meringues.
Cut the sponge cake in half and spread one half with the chestnut-meringue mixture. Replace the top.
Heat a little chestnut spread with some water to glaze the cake.

Strawberry sandwich cake

Serves 4–6
Preparation time: 30 minutes
Cooking time: 40 minutes

1 Genoese sponge cake (see page 66)
3 egg whites
200 g (7 oz) caster sugar
200 g (7 oz) butter
kirsch
225 g (8 oz) raspberry jelly
500 g (1 lb 2 oz) strawberries

Make a Genoese sponge cake in a deep sandwich tin, 22 cm (9 inches) in diameter. As soon as it is done, remove the cake from the tin and leave to cool.
Whisk the egg whites with the sugar in a bowl over a pan of hot water until the mixture resembles a shiny mousse.
Cream the butter and flavour it with a little kirsch. Gently fold the beaten egg whites into the butter cream.
Depending on the height of the sponge cake, slice it in 2 or 3 horizontally. Spread the bottom section with a layer of raspberry jelly, then a thicker layer of butter cream.
Cut the strawberries in half and arrange them on top of the butter cream. Cover with the second layer of cake. Spread with raspberry jelly, cream and fruit as before. Cover with the top layer of cake.
To decorate, coat the cake with the remaining butter cream and strawberries.

Lemon curd sandwich cake

Serves 4–6
Preparation time: 30 minutes
Cooking time: 40 minutes
Serves 4–6

1 Savoy sponge cake (see page 64)
3 egg whites
150 g (5 oz) sugar
100 g (4 oz) lemon curd
2 tablespoons poppy seeds
icing sugar
juice of 1 lemon

Make a Savoy sponge cake; remove it from the tin as soon as it is cooked.
Whisk the egg whites with the sugar over a bowl of hot water, until the mixture resembles a shiny mousse.
Beat the lemon curd with a spatula and gently fold it into the beaten egg whites together with 1 tablespoonful of poppy seeds.
Slice the sponge cake in two horizontally. Spread the base with the lemon mousse. Cover with the top layer.
Dilute a little icing sugar in some lemon juice. Pour it over the cake and sprinkle with the remaining poppy seeds.

Pound cake

This cake is infinitely variable depending on your taste and the contents of your cupboard! You simply weigh 3 eggs (in their shells) then weigh out the same amount of flour, sugar and butter.

Serves 4
Preparation time: 15 minutes
Cooking time: 35–40 minutes

1 deep sandwich tin, 22 cm (9 inches) in diameter

3 medium eggs weighing about 60 g (2 oz) each + 1 yolk
salted butter, cubed (at room temperature): the same weight as the eggs + 1 knob of butter
sugar: the same weight as the 3 eggs
plain flour: the same weight as the eggs
1 teaspoon baking powder

Preheat the oven to 150°C (300°F) Gas Mark 2. Thoroughly grease the tin with the knob of butter. Put the butter in a large basin and cream it with a spatula, then add the sugar and beat until the mixture turns pale and creamy. Add the eggs and yolk and mix well.
Quickly sift the flour and baking powder and fold into the contents of the basin.
The mixture should be completely smooth.
Pour into the sandwich tin and put in the oven. Leave to cook for about 40 minutes.
You can tell if it's done by piercing the centre of the cake with a knife: the blade should come out clean.
Allow the cake to cool before taking it out of the tin.

Orange pound cake

Serves 4
Preparation time: 15 minutes
Cooking time: 35–40 minutes

1 deep sandwich tin, 22 cm (9 inches) in diameter

3 medium eggs weighing about 60 g (2 oz) each + 1 yolk
salted butter, cubed (at room temperature): the same weight as the 3 eggs + 1 knob of butter
sugar: the same weight as the eggs
plain flour: the same weight as the eggs
1 teaspoon baking powder
2 teaspoons grated orange rind

Preheat the oven to 150°C (300°F) Gas Mark 2. Thoroughly grease the tin with the knob of butter. Put the rest of the butter in a large basin and cream it with a spatula, then add the sugar and beat until the mixture turns pale and creamy. Add the eggs and yolk and mix well.
Quickly sift the flour and baking powder into a large bowl and then pour them into the basin with the mixture.

Add the orange rind and mix again. The mixture should be completely smooth.
Pour it into the tin and put in the oven to cook for about 40 minutes.
You can tell if it's done by piercing the centre of the cake with a knife: the blade should come out clean.
Allow the cake to cool before taking it out of the tin.

Apple pound cake

Serves 4
Preparation time: 15 minutes
Cooking time: 35–40 minutes

1 deep sandwich tin, 22cm (9 inches) in diameter

2 good quality apples
juice of 1 lemon
3 medium eggs weighing about 60 g (2 oz) each + 1 yolk
salted butter, cubed (at room temperature): the same weight as the 3 eggs + 1 knob of butter for greasing the tin
sugar: the same weight as the eggs
plain flour: the same weight as the eggs
1 teaspoon baking powder

Preheat the oven to 150°C (300°F) Gas Mark 2. Thoroughly grease the tin with the knob of butter. Peel and quarter the apples and remove the cores and pips. Roughly chop the quarters and sprinkle them with the lemon juice.
Put the butter in a large basin and cream it with a spatula, then pour in the sugar and beat until the mixture becomes pale and creamy. Add the eggs and yolk and mix well.
Quickly sift and mix the flour and baking powder in a large bowl and pour them into the basin. The mixture should be completely smooth. Add the chopped apple and mix.
Pour the mixture into the tin and put in the oven to cook for about 40 minutes. You can tell if it's done by piercing the centre of the cake with a knife: the blade should come out clean.
Allow the cake to cool before taking it out of the tin.

Spice cake

Serves 6
Preparation time: 15 minutes
Cooking time: 50 minutes

1 loaf tin

20 g (¾ oz) butter for greasing the tin
100 ml (4 fl oz) milk
300 g (10½ oz) good quality runny honey
250 g (9 oz) wholemeal flour
2 teaspoons baking powder
50 g (2 oz) ground almonds
1 tablespoon ground mixed spices (cinnamon,
cloves, ginger and aniseed)
40 g (1½ oz) chopped candied orange peel
1 egg

Preheat the oven to 170°C (325°F) Gas Mark 3.
Grease the tin with the butter.
Gently heat the milk and honey together –
remove from the heat as soon as bubbles start to
form.
Sift the flour and baking powder together into a
bowl then mix in the ground almonds, spices and
chopped candied orange peel. Make a well in the
centre and then pour in the milk-honey mixture,
stirring all the time with a spoon. Finish by stirring
in the egg.
Pour the mixture into the tin and cook in the oven
for about 50 minutes.

Chocolate chip cake

Serves 4–6
Preparation time: 10 minutes
Cooking time: 40 minutes

1 square cake tin or a loaf tin

125 g (4½ oz) plain flour
1 teaspoon baking powder
80 g (3 oz) dark chocolate (at least 70% cocoa solids)
110 g (4 oz) salted butter (at room temperature), cubed + 20 g (¾ oz) for greasing the tin
120 g (4½ oz) icing sugar
2 tablespoons ground almonds
1 tablespoon cocoa powder
2 eggs
½ teaspoon vanilla extract
70 g (2½ oz) chocolate chips

Preheat the oven to 210°C (410°F) Gas Mark 6–7. Thoroughly grease the tin. Combine the flour and baking powder. Grate the dark chocolate.
Beat the butter and icing sugar with a wooden spoon until the mixture turns smooth and creamy. Gradually add the ground almonds, the flour-baking powder mixture, the cocoa powder, the grated chocolate and the eggs, stirring all the time.
Add the vanilla extract and the chocolate chips. Transfer the mixture to the tin, lower the temperature of the oven to 180°C (350°F), Gas Mark 4 and cook for about 40 minutes.
Serve warm or cold.
If you like you can sprinkle the cake with 2 or 3 tablespoons of rum when you take it out of the oven.

Easy bitter chocolate cake

Serves 4–6
Preparation time: 20 minutes
Cooking time: 30 minutes

1 round or square tart tin

200 g (7 oz) dark chocolate
4 eggs
1 pinch of salt
150 g (5 oz) salted butter, cubed (at room temperature) + 20 g (¾ oz) for greasing the tin
150 g (5 oz) sugar
50 g (2 oz) plain flour

Preheat the oven to 180°C (350°F) Gas Mark 4. Thoroughly grease the tin with the butter.
Half fill a pan with water and bring to the boil. Break the chocolate into pieces and put it to melt in a bowl resting over the pan (but not touching the water).
Break the eggs, separating the whites from the yolks. Beat the whites to form soft peaks, adding a pinch of salt.
Roughly combine the butter and sugar; add the melted chocolate, stirring all the time, then mix in the yolks, still stirring. Add the flour and finally the beaten egg whites in three stages. Mix gently until smooth.
Put the mixture into the tin, lower the oven temperature to 150°C (300°F), Gas Mark 2 and cook the cake for about 30 minutes.
Allow to cool slightly before removing it from the tin – it will be harder to take it out later on.

VARIATION • For a change you can always add some slivered almonds or small pieces of candied (crystallized) orange.

Easy bitter chocolate cake

Banana and rum cake

Serves 4–6
Preparation time: 20 minutes
Cooking time: 40 minutes

1 loaf tin

2 ripe bananas
juice of 1 lemon
1½ tablespoons rum
120 g (4½ oz) salted butter (at room
temperature), cubed + 20 g (¾ oz) for greasing
the tin
120 g (4½ oz) caster sugar
2 eggs
100 g (4 oz) chocolate (at least 70% cocoa solids)
250 g (9 oz) plain flour + 10 g (½ oz) for dusting
the tin
2 teaspoons baking powder
1 pinch of salt
1 teaspoon vanilla extract

Preheat the oven to 180°C (350°F) Gas Mark 4.
Thoroughly grease the tin and dust with flour.
Peel the bananas and mash them with a fork.
Pour the lemon juice and rum over the purée.
Beat the butter and sugar together in a large
bowl. As soon as the mixture turns pale, add the
eggs one at a time while continuing to beat.
Grate the chocolate.
In another bowl, mix the flour and baking
powder. Add the pinch of salt then pour into the
bowl containing the butter and sugar mixture.
Mix well then add the banana purée and vanilla
extract.
Put the mixture into the loaf tin and cook in the
oven for about 40 minutes.
For a stronger flavour sprinkle the cake with 3 or
4 tablespoons of rum when you take it out of the
oven.

Walnut cake

Serves 4–6
Preparation time: 15 minutes
Cooking time: 30 minutes

1 deep sandwich tin, about 22 cm (9 inches) in
diameter

4 eggs
100 g (4 oz) golden caster sugar
80 g (3 oz) salted butter + 20 g (¾ oz) for
greasing the tin
50 g (2 oz) plain flour + 10 g (½ oz) for dusting
the tin
170 g (6 oz) crushed walnut kernels
1 pinch of salt

Preheat the oven to 210°C (410°F) Gas Mark 6–7.
Grease the tin with the butter and dust lightly
with flour. Remove excess flour by tapping the
upturned tin.
Break the eggs, separating the whites from the
yolks. Mix the yolks with the sugar using a whisk.
Gently melt the butter in a small heavy-based
saucepan, then pour it into the egg-sugar
mixture. Mix well then gradually add the flour and
nut kernels.
Add the pinch of salt to the egg whites and beat
them into soft peaks. Fold them into the mixture
a little at a time using a wooden spoon so they
don't break down.
Spread mixture in the tin and cook for about 30
minutes. Allow to cool before removing it from
the tin.

VARIATION • You can use the same recipe to
make a hazelnut cake simply by substituting
hazelnuts for the walnuts.

Walnut cake

Banana and walnut cake

Serves 4–6
Preparation time: 15 minutes
Cooking time: 50 minutes

1 loaf tin

3 ripe bananas
220 g (8 oz) plain flour
1 teaspoon baking powder
100 g (4 oz) salted butter, cubed (at room temperature) + 20 g (¾ oz) for greasing the tin
100 g (4 oz) caster sugar
2 eggs
1 teaspoon vanilla extract
50 g (2 oz) chopped walnuts

Preheat the oven to 180°C (350°F) Gas Mark 4.
Grease the tin with the butter.
Peel the bananas and mash them with a fork.
Mix the flour and baking powder in a bowl.
Mix the bananas, butter, sugar, flour, eggs and vanilla extract in the bowl of your electric mixer then add the chopped walnuts. Spread the mixture in the tin and cook for about 50 minutes in the oven.
Allow to cool for about 10 minutes before taking the cake out of the tin.
This cake tastes even better the next day.

Hazelnut and honey cake

Serves 4–6
Preparation time: 10 minutes
Cooking time: 25 minutes

1 deep sandwich tin, 22 cm (9 inches) in diameter, or an assortment of small tins

3 eggs
1 pinch of salt
80 g (3 oz) caster sugar
40 g (1½ oz) plain flour
50 g (2 oz) chopped or ground hazelnuts
80 g (3 oz) butter + 20 g (¾ oz) for greasing the tin
50 g (2 oz) honey

Preheat the oven to 180°C (350°F) Gas Mark 4.
Grease the tin(s) with the butter.
Break the eggs, separating the whites from the yolks.
Add the pinch of salt to the egg whites and, using a whisk, beat them until they form stiff peaks.
In a large bowl mix the sugar, flour, egg yolks and chopped hazelnuts.
Melt the butter and honey in a heavy-based saucepan, then pour this mixture into the large bowl, stirring all the time.
Gently fold in the egg whites using a wooden spatula to avoid breaking down the whites.
Pour the mixture into the tin(s) and cook in the oven for about 25 minutes.
Allow the cake to cool before taking it out of the tin.

Hazelnut and honey cake

Carrot and sultana cake

Serves 4–6
Preparation time: 15 minutes
Cooking time: 45 minutes

1 loaf tin or deep sandwich cake tin

60 g (2½ oz) sultanas
3 tablespoons rum
4 eggs
120 g (4½ oz) salted butter, cubed (at room
temperature) + 20 g (¾ oz) for greasing the tin
350 g (12 oz) golden caster sugar
325 g (11½ oz) plain flour
2 teaspoons baking powder
400 g (14 oz) carrots, finely grated
1 teaspoon ground cinnamon
1 teaspoon ground ginger
¼ teaspoon grated nutmeg

Preheat the oven to 150°C (300°F) Gas Mark 2.
Thoroughly grease the tin with the butter.
Soak the sultanas in a bowl with the rum.
Whisk the eggs at high speed in a large bowl
then add the butter and sugar and blend until the
mixture turns creamy.
Mix the flour and the baking powder in another
bowl and pour into the butter-eggs-sugar mixture
in a stream. Add the carrots, sultanas soaked in
rum, cinnamon, ginger and nutmeg and mix well.
Pour into the tin and cook in the oven for about
45 minutes.
Allow to cool before taking the cake out of the
tin.
You can enjoy this cake warm or cold. It is
especially good the next day.

You can substitute 50 g (2 oz) pine kernels or
60 g (2½ oz) ground almonds for the sultanas if
you like.

Almond and carrot cake

Serves 4–6
Preparation time: 20 minutes
Cooking time: 40 minutes

1 loaf tin

20 g (¾ oz) butter for greasing the tin
5 eggs
120 g (4½ oz) plain flour + 10 g (½ oz) for
dusting the tin
180 g (6 oz) carrots, grated
250 g (9 oz) ground almonds
grated rind of 2 unwaxed oranges
120 g (4½ oz) golden caster sugar
1 pinch of salt

Preheat the oven to 210°C (410°F) Gas Mark 6–7.
Thoroughly grease the tin and dust with flour.
Break the eggs, separating the yolks from the
whites.
Mix together the flour, grated carrot, ground
almonds and grated orange rind in a large bowl.
Whisk the egg yolks and sugar in another bowl
then combine them with the ingredients in the
large bowl.
Add the pinch of salt to the egg whites and beat
them using your electric mixer (or a hand whisk)
until they form soft peaks. Gently fold them into
the mixture in the large bowl.
Cook in the oven for about 40 minutes.
Allow the cake to cool before taking it out of the
tin.
To serve, dust the cake with a little icing sugar.
You can enhance the flavour of your cake by
adding ½ teaspoon freshly milled cardamom seeds
to the mixture before cooking.

Carrot and sultana cake

Lemon and almond cake

Serves 4–6
Preparation time: 20 minutes
Cooking time: 40 minutes

1 loaf tin

200 g (7 oz) caster sugar
200 g (7 oz) salted butter (at room
temperature), cubed + 20 g (¾ oz) for greasing
the tin
200 g (7 oz) ground almonds
3 eggs
juice and rind of an unwaxed lemon
120 g (4½ oz) maize flour (or wholemeal flour)
+ 10 g (½ oz) for dusting the tin
1 teaspoon baking powder
1 pinch of salt

Preheat the oven to 180°C (350°F) Gas Mark 4.
Thoroughly grease the tin and dust with flour.
Beat the sugar and butter together in a large
bowl. When the mixture turns pale add the
ground almonds and then the eggs, one at a
time, and mix. Then add the lemon juice and rind.
In another bowl, mix the flour and baking
powder. Add the pinch of salt then add to the
bowl containing the butter, sugar, almonds, eggs
and lemon. Mix well.
Pour the mixture into the tin. Place the tin on a
baking sheet in the oven and cook for about 40
minutes.
Serve very fresh.

Marbled cake

Serves 4–6
Preparation time: 15 minutes
Cooking time: 30 minutes

1 loaf tin
1 cake rack

100 g (4 oz) salted butter (at room temperature), cubed + 20 g (¾ oz) for greasing the tin
100 g (4 oz) caster sugar
2 eggs
50 ml (2 fl oz) milk
200 g (7 oz) plain flour + 10 g (½ oz) for dusting the tin
1 teaspoon baking powder
1 pinch of salt
½ teaspoon vanilla sugar (see page 12)
1 tablespoon cocoa powder

Preheat the oven to 210°C (410°F) Gas Mark 6–7. Grease the tin with the butter and dust with flour. Using an electric whisk, beat the butter and sugar together until the mixture turns pale and frothy. Break the eggs, separating the whites from the yolks. Stir the yolks into the butter-sugar mixture, then add the milk, a little at a time, stirring as you pour.
Mix the flour and baking powder together in a large bowl then stir them into the mixture.
Add the pinch of salt to the whites and beat them into stiff peaks with an electric whisk.
Divide the mixture into 2 bowls.
Pour the vanilla sugar into the first and the cocoa powder into the second. Then gently fold half the egg whites into the vanilla flavoured mixture, using a spatula to mix in the whites without breaking them down. Fold the rest into the chocolate mixture.
Spread a layer of the vanilla mixture in the base of the tin then cover it with a layer of the chocolate. Repeat until the mixtures are used up.
Put the cake in the oven for 10 minutes then lower the heat to 180°C (350°F) Gas Mark 4 and cook for another 20 minutes.
Remove the cake from the tin and allow to cool on a cake rack.

Chestnut and vanilla cake

Serves 4–6
Preparation time: 15 minutes
Cooking time: 30 minutes

1 round tin (or charlotte mould if you have one)

3 eggs
1 pinch of salt
100 g (4 oz) salted butter + 20 g (¾ oz) for greasing the tin
500 g (1 lb 2 oz) pure chestnut purée
125 g (4½ oz) caster sugar
2 teaspoons vanilla extract

Preheat the oven to 180°C (350°F) Gas Mark 4. Grease the tin with butter.
Break the eggs, separating the whites from the yolks.
Add the pinch of salt to the whites and, using an electric mixer (or a hand whisk), beat until stiff white peaks form.
Slowly melt the butter in a small heavy-based saucepan.
In a large bowl blend the chestnut purée, egg yolks, sugar, melted butter and vanilla extract. Gently fold in the whites of egg using a spatula so they do not break down during the blending. Pour the mixture into the tin and smooth the surface with the spatula.
Put in the oven and cook for about 30 minutes. Allow the cake to cool before taking it out of the tin.

TIP • Serve very fresh with custard or double cream.

Marbled cake

Date and ginger cake

Serves 4–6
Preparation time: 10 minutes
Cooking time: 50 minutes

1 loaf tin

100 g (4 oz) stoned dates
250 g (9 oz) plain flour
1 teaspoon baking powder
180 g (6 oz) salted butter (at room temperature), cubed + 20 g (¾ oz) for greasing the tin
150 g (5 oz) caster sugar
2 eggs
1 teaspoon vanilla extract
200 ml (7 fl oz) milk
2 tablespoons chopped, preserved ginger

Preheat the oven to 180°C (350°F) Gas Mark 4. Grease the tin with the butter.
Chop the dates with a knife. Mix the flour and baking powder in a bowl.
In a large bowl, blend the butter and sugar, then add the flour in a stream. Blend in the eggs, chopped dates, vanilla extract and the milk, stirring all the time. Finally add the chopped preserved ginger.
Spread the mixture in the tin. Cook in the oven for about 50 minutes.
Allow to cool before taking the cake out of the tin.

Sultana and ginger cake

Serves 4–6
Preparation time: 20 minutes
Cooking time: 40 minutes

1 loaf tin

150 g (5 oz) sultanas
1 tablespoon rum
120 g (4½ oz) salted butter (at room temperature), cubed + 20 g (¾ oz) for greasing the tin
120 g (4½ oz) caster sugar
2 eggs
250 g (9 oz) plain flour + 10 g (½ oz) for dusting the tin
2 teaspoons baking powder
1 pinch of salt
1 tablespoon ground ginger

Put the sultanas to soak in a bowl with the rum.
Preheat the oven to 180°C (350°F) Gas Mark 4.
Thoroughly grease the tin and dust with flour.
Beat the butter and sugar together in a large bowl. When the mixture turns pale, gradually add the eggs, stirring all the time.
In another bowl, mix the flour with the baking powder.
Add the pinch of salt and ground ginger then pour the mixture into the bowl containing the butter and sugar. Blend well then add the sultanas.
Spread the mixture in the tin, place on a baking sheet and cook in the oven for about 40 minutes.

VARIATION • You can substitute candied orange peel for the sultanas.

Date and ginger cake

Fruit cake (with a difference)

Serves 4–6
Preparation time: 20 minutes
Cooking time: 45 minutes

1 loaf tin

80 g (3 oz) sultanas
1 tablespoon rum
120 g (4½ oz) salted butter (at room
temperature), cubed + 20 g (¾ oz) for greasing
the tin
120 g (4½ oz) caster sugar
2 eggs
250 g (9 oz) plain flour
2 teaspoons baking powder
150 g (5 oz) dried fruit (e.g. cherries, apricots,
figs), chopped

Put the sultanas in a bowl to soak with the rum.
Preheat the oven to 220°C (425°F) Gas Mark 7.
Thoroughly grease the loaf tin with the butter.
Cream the butter and caster sugar together in a
large bowl. When the mixture turns pale, add the
eggs one at a time, stirring constantly.
In another bowl, mix the flour and baking powder
then pour them into the butter mixture in a
stream, stirring vigorously with a spatula. Then stir
in the sultanas and chopped, dried fruit.
Spread the mixture in the tin; put the tin on a
baking sheet in the oven and cook for about 10
minutes. Then lower the temperature to 160°C
(325°F) Gas Mark 3 and cook for another 35
minutes.
Serve warm or cold at teatime.

Coconut and chocolate cake

Serves 4–6
Preparation time: 15 minutes
Cooking time: 45 minutes

1 loaf tin
1 cake rack

20 g (¾ oz) butter for greasing the tin
100 g (4 oz) dark chocolate
250 g (9 oz) plain flour
1 teaspoon baking powder
2 pinches of salt
3 eggs
100 g (4 oz) golden caster sugar
150 ml (5 fl oz) cooking oil (e.g. sunflower oil)
½ teaspoon vanilla extract
4 tablespoons milk
80 g (3 oz) + 2 tablespoons desiccated coconut
30 g (1 oz) cocoa powder

Preheat the oven to 180°C (350°F) Gas Mark 4.
Grease the tin with the butter. Grate the dark
chocolate.
Sift the flour and baking powder together into a
large bowl. Add a pinch of salt.
Break the eggs, separating the whites from the
yolks, and keep them in separate bowls.
Blend the sugar and egg yolks with a whisk.
Pour in the cooking oil, then the flour, stirring all
the time, and then the vanilla extract, the milk,
the 80 g (3 oz) desiccated coconut, the cocoa
powder and the grated chocolate.
Add the other pinch of salt to the egg whites and
beat them to form peaks, using a whisk. Gently
fold them into the mixture using a spatula,
making sure they don't break down.
Spread the mixture in the loaf tin. Sprinkle 2
spoonfuls desiccated coconut over the top.
Put in the oven. After 10 minutes, lower the oven
temperature to 150°C (300°F) Gas Mark 2 and
cook for another 35 minutes or so.
You can tell if it's done by piercing the centre with
a knife. The blade should come out clean.
Remove the cake from the tin and allow to cool
on a cake rack.

Green tea cake

Serves 4–6
Preparation time: 15 minutes
Cooking time: 40 minutes

1 loaf tin
1 cake rack

120 g (4 1/2 oz) plain flour
1 teaspoon baking powder
2 teaspoons green tea powder (available from
shops selling Chinese specialities)
2 eggs
100 g (4 oz) icing sugar
50 g (2 oz) ground almonds
100 g (4 oz) salted butter (at room
temperature), cubed + 20 g (¾ oz) for greasing
the tin
1 pinch of salt

Preheat the oven to 210°C (410°F) Gas Mark 6–7.
Grease the tin with the butter.
Mix the flour, baking powder and green tea
powder in a bowl.
Break the eggs, separating the yolks from the
whites. Blend the yolks and icing sugar together
in a large bowl then add the ground almonds.
Then add the cubed butter, blending until the
mixture turns smooth.
Put the pinch of salt in with the egg whites, then
beat them using the whisk part of your electric
mixer, until they form white peaks.
Add the flour then fold in the egg whites, a little
at a time.
Spread the mixture in the tin, put the tin in the
oven and lower the temperature to 160°C (325°F)
Gas Mark 3. Cook for about 40 minutes
When you take it out of the oven, wait about 10
minutes before removing the cake from the tin
and then leave to cool on a cake rack.

Cherry clafoutis

For me clafoutis is no ordinary dish – it takes me back to my childhood!

Serves 4–6
Preparation time: 10 minutes
Cooking time: 30 minutes

1 gratin dish

600 g (1 lb 5 oz) cherries
40 g (1½ oz) salted butter + 20 g (¾ oz) for greasing the dish
100 g (4 oz) plain flour
60 g (2 oz) caster sugar
1 pinch of salt
1 teaspoon vanilla sugar (see page 12)
4 eggs
200 ml (7 fl oz) milk
icing sugar for decoration

Preheat the oven to 210°C (410°F) Gas Mark 6–7.
Grease the dish generously with the butter.
Quickly wash the cherries under cold running water, remove the stalks and drain.
Melt the butter in a small heavy-based saucepan. Combine the flour, sugar, salt and vanilla sugar in a large bowl.
Break the eggs and blend them with the dry ingredients, a little at a time. Then gradually pour in the milk, still stirring. Add the melted butter. Arrange the cherries in the gratin dish and pour the mixture over them.
Bake for 10 minutes in the oven then lower the temperature to 180°C (350°F), Gas Mark 4 and cook for another 20 minutes.
Serve the cherry clafoutis warm or cold, with a dusting of icing sugar.

Pear clafoutis

Serves 4–6
Preparation time: 10 minutes
Cooking time: 30 minutes

1 gratin dish

4 ripe pears
40 g (1½ oz) salted butter + 20 g (¾ oz) for greasing the dish
100 g (4 oz) plain flour
60 g (2 oz) caster sugar
1 pinch of salt
1 pinch of ground cinnamon
1 heaped teaspoon vanilla sugar
4 eggs
200 ml (7 fl oz) milk
50 ml (2 fl oz) rum
icing sugar for decoration

Preheat the oven to 210°C (410°F) Gas Mark 6–7.
Wash the pears, peel and quarter them; remove the cores and pips then slice thinly.
Grease the dish with the butter and arrange the pear slices in the bottom.

Gently melt the butter in a small heavy-based saucepan.
Mix the flour, sugar, salt, ground cinnamon and vanilla sugar in a large bowl. Gradually add the whole eggs, then the milk, stirring continuously. Add the melted butter and the rum. The mixture should be quite smooth. Pour it over the pears.
Cook the clafoutis in the oven for 10 minutes, then lower the temperature to 180°C (350°F) Gas Mark 4 and cook for another 20 minutes.
Serve warm or cold, with a dusting of icing sugar.

Apricot clafoutis

Serves 4–6
Preparation time: 10 minutes
Cooking time: 30 minutes

1 gratin dish

600 g (1 lb 5 oz) apricots
40 g (1½ oz) salted butter + 20 g (¾ oz) for greasing the dish
100 g (4 oz) plain flour
60 g (2 oz) caster sugar
1 pinch of salt
1 pinch of ground ginger
1 heaped teaspoon vanilla sugar
4 eggs
200 ml (7 fl oz) milk
icing sugar for decoration

Preheat the oven to 210°C (410°F) Gas Mark 6–7.
Quickly wash the apricots, dry them with a tea towel, then cut them in half. Remove the stone.
Grease the dish with butter and arrange the apricot halves in it with the flat side facing down.
Gently melt the butter in a small heavy-based saucepan.
Mix the flour, sugar, salt, ginger and vanilla sugar in a large bowl. Gradually add the whole eggs and then the milk, stirring all the time. Finally add the melted butter. The mixture should be quite smooth. Pour it over the apricots.
Put the dish in the oven for 10 minutes, then lower the temperature to 180°C (350°F) Gas Mark 4 and cook for another 20 minutes.
Serve the apricot clafoutis warm or cold, with a dusting of icing sugar.

Cherry clafoutis

Breton buttercake (Kouign amann)

Literally 'bread and butter' cake – from Brittany. The secret of a good kouign amann is butter, butter and yet more butter – and pastry made with bread dough!

Serves 4–6
Preparation time: 10 minutes + 1 hour (for the dough) and 3 x 30 minutes
Cooking time: 30 minutes

1 deep sandwich tin, 28 cm (about 11 inches) in diameter

For the dough:
½ sachet dried yeast
25 ml (1 fl oz) warm water
a pinch of sugar
200 g (7 oz) plain flour
For the buttercake:
120 g (4½ oz) salted butter (at room temperature)
110 g (4 oz) caster sugar + 20 g (¾ oz) for decoration

In a large bowl dissolve the yeast in the warm water with a pinch of sugar (or follow the manufacturer's directions on the packet). Sprinkle the flour onto the dissolved yeast and mix to a smooth dough. Cover with a tea towel and leave in a warmish place until it doubles in volume (about 1 hour).
Flatten the dough on your work surface to form a large square. Spread the butter on the dough and dust with sugar. Bring the edges of the dough in towards the centre, over the butter and sugar.
Roll out the dough again with a rolling pin to make a rectangular shape this time. Fold the bottom third into the centre and the top third over the bottom third. Leave for 30 minutes. Turn the dough through 90° and flatten with the rolling pin. Fold in three again and leave for another 30 minutes.
Turn the pastry through 90° again, fold it and flatten it with the rolling pin and leave for a further 30 minutes.
Preheat the oven to 210°C (410°F) Gas Mark 6–7. Grease the tin.
Using your rolling pin, form the dough into a circle to fit the tin. Put it into the tin, sprinkle it with a little water and dust with caster sugar. Cook in the oven for 30 minutes.
Serve warm.

Breton egg plumcake (Far breton)

Serves 4–6
Preparation time: 15 minutes
Cooking time: 30 minutes

1 gratin dish

750 ml (just over 1¼ pints) milk
1 vanilla pod
180 g (6 oz) prunes, stoned
4 tablespoons plain flour
100 g (4 oz) caster sugar
4 eggs
50 g (2 oz) salted butter + ¾ oz for greasing the dish
1 tablespoon rum

Preheat the oven to 210°C (410°F) Gas Mark 6–7.
Grease an ovenproof dish.
Pour the milk into a heavy-based saucepan. Split
the vanilla pod lengthways and put it in the milk.
Bring the milk to the boil and immediately take
the pan off the heat. Using the point of a knife,
scrape the vanilla seeds from inside the pod and
put them in the pan along with the empty pod.
Leave to infuse as the liquid cools at room
temperature.
Arrange the stoned prunes in the dish.
Mix the flour and sugar in a large bowl.
Remove the vanilla pod from the milk, break the
eggs and add them to the milk. Whisk and then
add this mixture to the bowl containing the flour
and sugar. Melt the butter in a small saucepan
and add it to the mixture, with the rum.
Pour the mixture into the dish and cook for about
30 minutes. The cake should turn a nice golden
colour.
Serve warm or chilled.

TIP • If you would like to soften your prunes and
enhance their flavour, soak them for 20 minutes
beforehand in a little warm water mixed with
rum.

Austrian yeast cake (Kugelhopf)

The secret of a good Kugelhopf lies in the temperature of the ingredients – they must all be at room temperature when you use them. Ideally you should use a proper Kugelhopf mould but don't worry if you haven't got one – you can get excellent results with an ordinary ring mould.

Serves 4–6
Preparation time: 15 minutes
Cooking time: 50 minutes

1 ring mould

60 g (2 oz) sultanas
1 tablespoon water + 2 tablespoons warm water
1 tablespoon kirsch liqueur
1 sachet dried yeast
300 g (10½ oz) plain flour
60 g (2 oz) caster sugar
½ teaspoon salt
150 ml (5 fl oz) milk
1 egg
100 g (4 oz) salted butter, cubed, at room temperature + 20 g (¾ oz) for greasing the mould

Thoroughly grease the mould with the butter. Soak the sultanas in the kirsch and 1 tablespoon water in a bowl.
Mix the yeast in 2 tablespoons warm water and leave to swell for about 10 minutes (or follow the directions on the packet).
Put the flour, sugar, salt, milk, yeast and the egg in the bowl of your food processor and blend vigorously (or use a hand whisk). Add the cubed butter and continue blending until the mixture forms a smooth pliable dough. Add the sultanas and mix well.
Spread the dough in the mould, cover with a tea towel and leave to rise for about 3 hours at room temperature.
Preheat the oven to 210°C (410°F) Gas Mark 6–7. Put the mould in the oven, immediately lower the temperature to 180°C (350°F) Gas Mark 4, and leave to cook for about 50 minutes. Remove the Kugelhopf from the mould and serve cold with coffee or hot chocolate.

TIP • For decoration, you can sprinkle 50 g (2 oz) whole almonds inside the buttered mould before you put in the dough.

Brioche with pink pralines

Serves 4–6
Preparation time: 25 minutes
Cooking time: 40 minutes

1 loaf tin or brioche mould

1 sachet dried yeast
50 ml (2 fl oz) warm milk
250 g (9 oz) plain flour
2 medium eggs + 1 yolk
2 tablespoons caster sugar
125 g (4½ oz) salted butter (at room
temperature), cubed + 20 g (¾ oz) for greasing
the tin
100 g (4 oz) pink pralines (candied rose petals)

Dissolve the yeast in the warm milk (or follow the
directions on the packet). Pour the flour, eggs,
sugar and yeast mixed with milk into your food
processor. Blend on medium speed (or use a hand
whisk) then add the cubed butter. Blend again
until the mixture is completely smooth.
Form the dough into a ball and put it in a warm
place (next to a radiator for instance) covered
with a tea towel. Leave it until it doubles in
volume (at least 1 hour) then add the pink
pralines and knead by hand for a few minutes.
Grease the tin with the butter and put the dough
into the tin. Cover once more with the tea towel
and leave to rise for 1 hour in a warm place.
Preheat the oven to 180°–190°C (350°–375°F)
Gas Mark 4–5.
Put the brioche in the oven and cook for about
40 minutes. Ten minutes before the end of the
cooking time, lower the oven temperature slightly
to prevent the brioche burning on the bottom.
Allow to cool slightly before taking the brioche
out of the tin.

Butter brioche

Serves 4–6
Preparation time: 20 minutes
Cooking time: 40 minutes

1 loaf tin or brioche mould

1 sachet dried yeast
50 ml (2 fl oz) warm milk
250 g (9 oz) plain flour
2 medium eggs + 1 yolk
2 tablespoons caster sugar
125 g (4½ oz) salted butter (at room
temperature), cubed + 20 g (¾ oz) for greasing
the tin

Dissolve the yeast in the warm milk (or follow the
directions on the packet). Pour the flour, eggs,
sugar and yeast in milk into your food processor.
Blend on medium speed (or use a hand whisk)
then add the cubed butter. Blend again until the
mixture is completely smooth.
Form the dough into a ball and put it in a warm
place (next to a radiator for instance) covered
with a tea towel. Leave until it doubles in volume
(at least 1 hour) then knead by hand for a few
minutes.
Grease the tin with the butter and put the dough
into the tin. Cover once more with the tea towel
and leave to rise for 1 hour in a warm place.
Preheat the oven to 180°–190°C (350°–375°F)
Gas Mark 4–5.
Put the brioche in the oven and cook for about
40 minutes. Ten minutes before the end of the
cooking time, lower the oven temperature slightly
to prevent the brioche burning on the bottom.
Allow to cool slightly before taking the brioche
out of the tin.

Apple pie

Serves 4–6
Preparation time: 15 minutes
Cooking time: 35 minutes

1 deep sandwich tin approximately 22 cm (9 inches) in diameter

20 g (¾ g) butter for greasing the tin
500 g (1 lb 2 oz) shortcrust pastry
1.2 kg (2 lb 8 oz) good quality eating apples
(e.g. Cox's Orange Pippins)
3 tablespoons golden caster sugar
1 teaspoon ground cinnamon
1 teaspoon ground ginger
½ teaspoon grated nutmeg
juice of 1 lemon

Preheat the oven to 210°C (410°F) Gas Mark 6–7. Grease the tin with butter.
Peel and quarter the apples, remove the cores and pips, then slice thickly into a large bowl.
Mix the sugar, cinnamon, ginger and nutmeg together in a small bowl then sprinkle over the apples. Make sure that each piece is dusted with spiced sugar. Moisten with lemon juice.
Roll out two-thirds of the pastry on a floured work surface, using a rolling pin. Lift the pastry into the tin, allowing it to hang over the sides. Lightly prick the pastry base with a fork. Arrange the slices of spiced apple on top. Roll out the rest of the dough into a circle and place over the apples. Gently press the two thicknesses of pastry together with the fingers. Make a small hole in the centre of the pastry (to permit steam to escape during cooking) and put it in the oven for 35 minutes.

TIPS • Serve warm or cold, with vanilla ice cream or a little cream.
The quantity of sugar used in this recipe depends on the acidity of your apples. Taste one raw before you add the sugar!
You can also make delicious pear or rhubarb pies following the same recipe – substituting pears or rhubarb for the apples.

Cream cheese cake

Serves 4–6
Preparation time: 15 minutes
Cooking time: 15 minutes + 35 minutes

1 deep sandwich tin about 22 cm (9 inches) in diameter
some dried haricot beans

20 g (¾ oz) butter for greasing the tin
shortcrust pastry (for the base of the tin) (see page 14)
6 eggs
150 g (5 oz) caster sugar
400g (14 oz) cream cheese
½ teaspoon vanilla extract
1 pinch of salt
icing sugar

Preheat the oven to 180°C (350°F) Gas Mark 4.
Grease the tin and line with shortcrust pastry, pressing the edges down firmly with the fingertips and forming a little lip of pastry. Prick the pastry lightly with a fork. Cover with a layer of dried haricot beans and cook for 15 minutes in the oven.
Meanwhile break the eggs and separate the whites from the yolks. Then mix the sugar and egg yolks in a large bowl. Add the cream cheese and vanilla extract.
Add the salt to the egg whites in another bowl and beat them with your electric whisk until they form stiff peaks.
Gently fold the egg whites into the cream cheese mixture with a spatula.
Pour the mixture into the precooked pastry case and put in the oven for about 35 minutes.
Remove from the tin and leave to cool on a rack.
Dust the cream cheese cake with a little icing sugar before serving.

Cheesecake

Serves 6
Preparation time: 10 minutes
Cooking time: 35 minutes

1 deep sandwich tin 22 cm (9 inches) in diameter

200 g (7 oz) ginger biscuits
60 g (2 oz) butter (at room temperature), cubed
600 g (1 lb 5 oz) fresh cream cheese
200 ml (7 fl oz) double cream
1 pinch of salt
180 g (6 oz) caster sugar
3 eggs
1 tablespoon maple syrup
1 teaspoon vanilla extract
1 teaspoon ground cinnamon

Preheat the oven to 150°C (300°F) Gas Mark 2.
Crush the biscuits and mix them with the butter.
Press the mixture well into the base of the tin.
Beat the cream cheese and cream and add the salt, sugar, eggs one at a time, maple syrup, vanilla extract and cinnamon.
Pour the mixture into the tin and cook in the oven for about 35 minutes.
Loosen the sides by running a knife blade between the tin and the cheesecake; leave to cool, then chill for at least 2 hours.
This cheesecake can be made the day before.

Tarts, charlottes, etc.

Tropical fruit tart

Serves 4–6
Preparation time: 20 minutes
Cooking time: 15 minutes

1 tart tin about 26 cm (10 inches) in diameter
dried beans
1 cake rack

20 g (¾ oz) butter for greasing the tin
300 g (10½ oz) shortcrust pastry (see page 14)
2 bananas
3 kiwi fruit
1 fresh pineapple
300 ml (10 fl oz) single cream
250 g (9 oz) crème pâtissière (see page 18)

Preheat the oven to 180°C (350°F) Gas Mark 4.
Thoroughly grease the tin.
Roll the pastry and cut out a circle to line the tin.
Prick the base lightly with a fork and cover with a
sheet of greaseproof paper. Sprinkle some dried
beans on top and cook for about 15 minutes.
Meanwhile prepare the fruit. Peel them; slice the
bananas and kiwi fruit and cut the pineapple into
cubes.
Take the cream out of the refrigerator and whisk
lightly. Fold it into the crème pâtissière.
Remove the pastry base from the oven when
done, take it out of the tin and leave to cool on a
rack.
Spread a layer of crème pâtissière over the pastry
and arrange the fruit on top.

TIP • To make this tart even more delicious you
could heat 30 g (1 oz) apple jelly with a
tablespoon of water and use it to glaze the fruit
with a brush.

Lemon tart

Serves 4–6
Preparation time: 25 minutes
Cooking time: 20 minutes

1 tart tin 26 cm (10 inches) in diameter
dried beans

300 g (10½ oz) sweet flan pastry (see page 14)
4 sheets of gelatine (agar-agar)
juice and rind of 4 unwaxed lemons
400 g (14 oz) caster sugar
8 fresh eggs
250 g (9 oz) salted butter (at room
temperature), cubed + 20 g (¾ oz) for greasing
the tin

Preheat the oven to 180°C (350°F) Gas Mark 4.
Put the sheets of gelatine to soak in a bowl of
cold water.
Grease the tin with the butter. Roll out the pastry
and line the tin with it.
Prick the pastry base lightly with a fork and cover
with a sheet of greaseproof paper. Sprinkle some
dried beans on top and cook for 10 to 12
minutes.
Beat the eggs.
Remove the dried beans and the greaseproof
paper, glaze the pastry with a little of the beaten
egg and put back in the oven for another
5 minutes or so. This will keep the pastry crisp
when filled with the lemon cream. Take the tart
base out of the tin and leave to cool on a rack.
Pour the juice and rind of the lemons, caster
sugar, eggs and cubed butter into a heavy-based
saucepan. Mix well and boil for 1 minute. Add
the gelatine leaves, whisk and pour the mixture
into the tart base.
Leave to cool before serving.

Lemon tart

Apricot and almond tart

Serves 4–6
Preparation time: 35 minutes
Cooking time: 30 minutes

1 tart tin approximately 26 cm (10 inches) in
diameter
dried beans

1 pinch of salt
50 ml (2 fl oz) cold water + 50 ml (2 fl oz) for
cooking the apricots
250 g (9 oz) plain flour
10 g (1/2 oz) sugar
100 ml (4 fl oz) cooking oil
1 tablespoon orange flower water
20 g (3/4 oz) butter for greasing the tin
10 apricots
1 tablespoon honey
100 g (4 oz) ground almonds
50 g (2 oz) flaked almonds

First make the pastry: dissolve the salt in 50 ml
(2 fl oz) cold water. Mix the flour with the sugar
and oil. Add the salted water and the orange
flower water and knead the pastry with the
fingertips. Cover with clingfilm and leave in the
refrigerator for at least 1 hour.
Preheat the oven to 180°C (350°F) Gas Mark 4.
Lightly grease the tin with the butter. Line it with
the pastry and prick lightly with a fork. Cover
with a circle of greaseproof paper and a layer of
dried beans. Put the tart base in the oven for
about 15 minutes.
Meanwhile, wash the apricots, dry them, cut
them in half and remove the stones.
Pour the water and honey into a frying pan.
Carefully place the apricot halves in the water and
cook them for about 15 minutes, turning them
over half way through.
Take the pastry base out of the tin and leave to
cool, then cover with a layer of ground almonds.
Place the halved, cooked apricots face down in
the base. Sprinkle with flaked almonds and serve
immediately.

TIP • You don't need to wait for the summer to
make this tart. You can always use frozen
apricots.

Plum tart with cinnamon

If you can get it, the Alsatian quetsch is a wonderful plum for cooking. It gives off a subtle aroma of caramel when ripe. You could also use the Czar or Kirke's Blue varieties.

Serves 4–6
Preparation time: 20 minutes
Cooking time: 35 minutes

1 tart tin about 26 cm (10 inches) in diameter

250 g (9 oz) shortcrust pastry (see page 14)
20 g (¾ oz) butter for greasing the tin
1.2 kg (2 lb 12 oz) plums
120 g (4½ oz) ground almonds
80 g (3 oz) golden caster sugar
½ teaspoon ground cinnamon

Preheat the oven to 180°C (350°F) Gas Mark 4. Grease the tin and line it with the pastry. Pinch the edges with your fingers. Lightly prick the tart base with a fork. Cover with a layer of clingfilm and put in the refrigerator for about 15 minutes. Wash the plums, dry them thoroughly, then cut them in half and remove the stones.
Sprinkle a layer of ground almonds in the tart base and arrange the plums on top, cut face up. Mix the sugar and cinnamon in a bowl, then sprinkle this spicy mixture over the plums.
Cook for about 35 minutes. Remove from the tin and allow the tart to cool a little.
Serve with vanilla ice cream.

Upside-down cake (Tarte Tatin)

This upside-down cake has many different versions. Here are three to choose from. You can also make up your own but apple tarte Tatin made with cooking apples will always be the best.

Upside-down cake (Tarte Tatin) – with apples

Serves 4–6
Preparation time: 10 minutes
Cooking time: 30 minutes

1 deep flan dish about 22 cm (9 inches) in diameter

300 g (10½ oz) shortcrust pastry (see page 14)
1 kg (2 lb 4 oz) cooking apples
100 g (4 oz) caster sugar
3 tablespoons water
vinegar
40 g (1½ oz) salted butter (at room temperature), cubed (for the caramel) + 20 g (¾ oz) for greasing the tin + 20 g (¾ oz) for the apples

Preheat the oven to 240°C (475°F) Gas Mark 9. Grease the dish with butter.
Peel and quarter the apples, remove the cores and pips. Cut them into chunks.

Make the caramel: slowly dissolve 50 g (2 oz) sugar with 3 tablespoons water in a small heavy-based saucepan. Then turn up the heat and boil until the mixture turns golden; add 2 or 3 drops of white or malt vinegar and 40 g (1½ oz) butter. Take off the heat, stir and pour into the buttered dish.
Arrange the apple chunks in the dish, rounded side down, and dot with butter. Dust with the remaining sugar.
Roll the pastry out to form a large circle, place it on top of the apples and tuck in the edges. Cook for about 25 minutes.

TIP • Serve the tart warm or reheat it slightly. If you reheat it in a microwave, do not leave it in too long as the pastry may lose its crispness. Always serve with a small jug of cream for each guest.

Upside-down cake (Tarte Tatin) – with mangoes

Serves 4–6
Preparation time: 10 minutes
Cooking time: 30 minutes

1 deep flan dish about 22 cm (9 inches) in diameter

300 g (10½ oz) shortcrust pastry (see page 14)
1 kg (2 lb 4 oz) mangoes
100g (4 oz) caster sugar
3 tablespoons water
vinegar
40 g (1½ oz) salted butter (at room
temperature), cubed (for the caramel) + 20 g
(¾ oz) for the mangoes

Preheat the oven to 240°C (475°F) Gas Mark 9.
Grease the dish with butter.
Peel the mangoes, remove the stones and cut into
slices.
Make the caramel: slowly dissolve 50 g (2 oz)
sugar with 3 tablespoons water in a small heavy-
based saucepan. Then turn up the heat and boil
until the mixture turns golden; add 2 or 3 drops
of white or malt vinegar and 40 g (1½ oz) butter.
Take off the heat, stir and pour into the buttered
dish.
Arrange the mangoes in the dish on top of the
caramel. Dust with the remaining sugar and dot
with the cubed butter.
Roll the pastry to form a large circle; place it on
top of the mangoes and tuck in the edges. Cook
for about 25 minutes.
Serve warm.

Upside-down cake (Tarte Tatin) – with pears

Serves 4–6
Preparation time: 10 minutes
Cooking time: 30 minutes

1 deep flan dish about 22 cm (9 inches) in diameter

300 g (10½ oz) shortcrust pastry (see page 14)
1 kg (2 lb 4 oz) firm pears
100g (4 oz) caster sugar
3 tablespoons water
vinegar
40 g (1½ oz) salted butter (at room temperature),
cubed (for the caramel) + 20 g (¾ oz) for the
pears

Preheat the oven to 240°C (475°F) Gas Mark 9.
Grease the dish with the butter.
Peel and quarter the pears, remove the cores and
pips. Cut them into chunks.
Make the caramel: slowly dissolve 50 g (2 oz)
sugar with 3 tablespoons water in a small heavy-
based saucepan. Then turn up the heat and boil
until the mixture turns golden; add 2 or 3 drops
of white or malt vinegar and 40 g (1½ oz) butter.
Remove from the heat, stir and pour into the
buttered dish.
Arrange the pear chunks in the dish, rounded side
down, and dot with butter. Dust with the
remaining sugar.
Roll the pastry out to form a large circle, place it
on top of the pears and tuck in the edges. Cook
for about 25 minutes.
Serve warm.

Pear tarte Tatin

Strawberry tart

Some good quality shortcrust pastry, some tasty strawberries and some home-made crème Chantilly! It's as easy as that. Sheer bliss!

Serves 4–6
Preparation time: 15 minutes
Cooking time: 15 minutes

1 tart tin about 26 cm (10 inches) in diameter
dried beans
1 cake rack

shortcrust pastry (see page 14)
20 g (¾ oz) butter for greasing the tin
500 g (just over 1 lb) strawberries
200 ml (7 fl oz) double cream
½ teaspoon vanilla sugar

Preheat the oven to 180°C (350°F) Gas Mark 4. Thoroughly grease the tin.
Roll out the pastry to form a large circle and line the tin with it. Make a little rim all around. Lightly prick the base with a fork, cover it with a sheet of greaseproof paper and place some dried beans on top. Cook for about 15 minutes.
When cooked but not coloured, take the pastry base out of the oven; remove the greaseproof paper and the dried beans. Take the base out of the tin and leave to cool on a rack.
Prepare the strawberries: wash them quickly under cold running water, drain and hull them. Cut them in half. Arrange the strawberries on the pastry base, cut side up.

Crème Chantilly

See recipe page 22.

Decorate the tart with blobs of cream. You can use an icing bag if you like. Serve immediately.

Raspberry tart

Make your pastry base exactly as for the strawberry tart. Make the crème Chantilly in advance and keep it in the refrigerator.
Just before serving spread a layer of crème Chantilly in the pastry base and arrange the fresh raspberries on top.

VARIATIONS • According to the season, you can replace the raspberries with blackberries or blackcurrants. Not only are these tarts good to eat – they look pretty too.
You can often find good quality frozen fruit in specialist shops. Remember to thaw it well in advance.

Austrian shortbread (Linzertorte)

Serves 4–6
Preparation time: 20 minutes
Cooking time: 30 minutes

1 tart tin about 26 cm (10 inches) in diameter

125 g (4½ oz) plain flour
1 pinch of salt
1 egg
125 g (4½ oz) salted butter (at room temperature), cubed + 20 g (¾ oz) for greasing the tin
125 g (4½) caster sugar
125 g (4½ oz) ground almonds
grated rind of ¼ unwaxed lemon
1 teaspoon ground cinnamon
1 teaspoon cocoa powder
150 g (5 oz) raspberry jam
½ glass milk

Sift the flour onto the work surface and make a well in the middle. Put the salt, egg, butter and sugar in the well. Mix using your fingertips then add the ground almonds, lemon rind, cinnamon and cocoa powder. Gradually blend in the flour then quickly work the pastry between the thumbs and fingertips until it takes on a sandy texture.
Roll it into a ball, wrap it in clingfilm and put it in the refrigerator for at least 1 hour.
Preheat the oven to 180°C (350°F) Gas Mark 4. Grease the tin.
Roll two-thirds of the pastry out into a circle, roll it round the rolling pin and press it gently into the tin.
Spread the jam over the pastry base then roll out the rest of the pastry and cut it into strips 1 cm (½ inch) wide (as illustrated above left). Arrange the strips in a lattice over the jam. Glaze with a little milk and cook for 30 minutes.
Serve cold with whipped cream. The pastry is best if made the day before.

Almond tartlets

Makes 8 tartlets
Preparation time: 15 minutes
Cooking time: 20 minutes

tartlet tins 10 cm (4 inches) in diameter

300 g (10½ oz) shortcrust pastry (see page 14)
120 g (4½ oz) ground almonds
3 eggs
25 g salted butter (at room temperature), cubed
+ 20 g (¾ oz) for greasing the tins
30 g (1 oz) caster sugar
1 tablespoon rum

Preheat the oven to 180°C (350°F) Gas Mark 4.
Thoroughly grease the tins with the butter.
Mix the ground almonds with the eggs, butter,
sugar and rum.
Roll out the shortcrust pastry and cut into circles
about 14 cm (6 inches) in diameter.
Put a circle of pastry into each tin, gently pressing
it in with the fingers. Then prick the base of each
tartlet with a fork.
Spread the almond mixture over the pastry and
cook for about 20 minutes.
If you like, you can decorate the tartlets with
flaked roasted almonds.

Apple crumble

Serves 4–6
Preparation time: 15 minutes
Cooking time: 35 minutes

1 gratin dish

1.2 kg (2 lb 12 oz) apples
4 tablespoons calvados
100 g (4 oz) wholemeal flour (or half
wholemeal, half plain white flour)
50 g (2 oz) ground almonds
1 teaspoon ground cinnamon
120 g (4½ oz) golden caster sugar
100 g (4 oz) salted butter (at room
temperature), cubed + 20 g (¾ oz) for greasing
the dish
1 pinch of salt

Preheat the oven to 180°C (350°F) Gas Mark 4.
Grease the dish with butter.
Peel and quarter the apples, remove the cores and
pips and slice coarsely.
Put the apples on a deep plate and drizzle with
calvados.
Mix the flour, ground almonds, cinnamon, sugar
and butter in a large bowl. Add the pinch of salt.
Stir gently.
Arrange the apple slices soaked in calvados in the
dish. Cover with the flour-ground-almond-butter-
sugar mixture and cook for about 35 minutes
Serve warm or cold.

Red fruit crumble

Serves 4–6
Preparation time: 15 minutes
Cooking time: 25 minutes

1 gratin dish

800 g (1 lb 12 oz) red fruit (raspberries, redcurrants, blackcurrants, blackberries etc.)
100 g (4 oz) plain flour
100 g (4 oz) golden caster sugar
50 g (2 oz) ground almonds
½ teaspoon ground cinnamon
100 g (4 oz) salted butter (at room temperature), cubed + 20 g (¾ oz) for greasing the dish
1 pinch of salt
grated rind of ½ an unwaxed lemon

Preheat the oven to 180°C (350°F) Gas Mark 4. Grease the dish with butter.
Pick over the fruit then wash it quickly under cold running water and drain.
Combine the flour, sugar, ground almonds, cinnamon and butter in a large bowl.
Add the pinch of salt. Rub together with the fingertips until the mixture resembles breadcrumbs.
Sprinkle the lemon rind over the base of the dish and arrange the red fruits on top. Cover with the flour-sugar-ground-almond-cinnamon-butter mixture and cook for about 25 minutes.
Serve warm or cold.

Rhubarb and apple crumble

Serves 4–6
Preparation time: 15 minutes
Cooking time: 25 minutes

1 gratin dish

3 apples
1 kg (2 lb 4 oz) rhubarb cut into chunks
100 g (4 oz) golden caster sugar for the fruit + 80 g (3 oz) for the crumble
½ teaspoon ground ginger
120 g (4½ oz) plain flour
100 g (4 oz) salted butter (at room temperature), cubed + 20 g (¾ oz) for greasing the dish
1 pinch of salt

Preheat the oven to 180°C (350°F) Gas Mark 4. Grease the dish with butter.
Peel and quarter the apples, remove the cores and pips and slice coarsely. Put the slices in a large bowl with the prepared rhubarb, sugar and ginger. Mix well.
Combine the flour, the remaining 80 g (3 oz) sugar and butter in a large bowl. Add the pinch of salt. Rub together with the fingertips until the mixture resembles breadcrumbs.
Arrange the apples and rhubarb in the dish. Cover with the flour-butter-sugar mixture and cook for about 25 minutes.
Serve warm or cold.
For a pleasant nutty flavour, try using wholemeal flour.

Rhubarb and apple crumble

Red fruit crumble

Mango and cinnamon charlotte

Make the day before
Serves 4–6
Preparation time: 15 minutes
Cooking time: 20 minutes

1 charlotte mould with removable lid or a straight-sided glass dish

800 g (1 lb 12 oz) mangoes (fresh or tinned)
30 g (1 oz) salted butter
80 g (3 oz) caster sugar + 50 g (2 oz) for the caramel
½ teaspoon ground cinnamon
4 tablespoons water
250 ml (9 fl oz) milk
30 sponge fingers

The day before, peel the mangoes, remove the stones and chop the flesh.
Melt the butter in a nonstick frying pan and use it to cook the chopped mango on a medium heat for a few minutes. Pour in 80 g (3 oz) sugar and cook on a low heat for about 12 minutes. Then add the ground cinnamon and mix well.
Make the caramel: melt 50 g (2 oz) sugar with 2 tablespoons water in a small heavy-based saucepan. Then boil rapidly until the caramel turns a golden colour. Remove from the heat and pour in 2 tablespoons of water. Leave to cool then add the milk.
Quickly dip the sponge fingers in the caramelized milk and use them to line the base and sides of the mould.
Put a layer of mango in the base and cover it with dipped fingers; fill the mould with alternate layers, finishing with a layer of fingers.
Serve with custard, if you like.
You could use tinned mangoes instead of fresh ones.

Pear charlotte

Make the day before
Serves 4–6
Preparation time: 15 minutes
Cooking time: 20 minutes

1 charlotte mould with removable lid or a straight-sided glass dish

800 g (1 lb 12 oz) pears
30 g (1 oz) salted butter
80 g (3 oz) caster sugar + 50 g (2 oz) for the caramel
2 heaped teaspoons vanilla sugar
2 tablespoons water
250 ml (9 fl oz) milk
30 sponge fingers

The day before, peel and quarter the pears, remove the cores and pips and slice.
Melt the butter in a nonstick frying pan and use it to cook the pears on medium heat for a few minutes. Pour in the 80 g (3 oz) caster sugar and the vanilla sugar and cook on a very low heat for about 12 minutes.
Make the caramel: melt 50 g (2 oz) sugar with 2 tablespoons water in a small heavy-based saucepan. Then boil rapidly until the caramel turns a golden colour. Remove from the heat and pour in 2 tablespoons of water. Leave to cool then add the milk.
Quickly dip the sponge fingers in the caramelized milk and use them to line the base and sides of the mould. Put a layer of pears in the bottom and cover them with dipped fingers. Continue with alternate layers until the mould is full, finishing with a layer of fingers.
Cover the mould and put it in the refrigerator overnight. Take the charlotte out of the mould and serve very cold.
If you like, you can pour on some hot caramel, just before serving.

Pear charlotte

Red fruit charlotte

Make the day before
Serves 4–6
Preparation time: 15 minutes
No cooking required

1 charlotte mould with removable lid or a straight-sided glass dish

30 sponge fingers
150 ml (5 fl oz) orange juice
400 g (14 oz) fromage frais
80 g (3 oz) caster sugar
2 heaped teaspoons vanilla sugar (see page 12)
300 g (10½ oz) raspberries and strawberries
a few blackcurrants for decoration

Quickly dip the sponge fingers in the orange juice. Use them to line the base and sides of the mould. Whisk the fromage frais, sugar and vanilla sugar in a bowl.
Quickly wash the raspberries and strawberries under cold running water and drain them. Put half the red fruit in the mould and cover with half the sweetened fromage frais. Add a layer of sponge fingers followed by the remaining red fruit and fromage frais. Finish with a layer of sponge fingers.
Cover and chill in the refrigerator overnight. Remove from the mould and serve very cold.

Chocolate charlotte

Make the day before
Serves 4–6
Preparation time: 15 minutes
No cooking required

1 charlotte mould with removable lid or a straight-sided glass dish

600 g (1 lb 5 oz) dark chocolate mousse (see page 150)
1 mug of black coffee
3 tablespoons brandy
30 sponge fingers

The day before, pour the coffee and brandy into a shallow dish. Quickly dip the fingers into the liquid and use them to line the base and sides of the mould.
Fill with chocolate mousse and top with a layer of fingers.
Cover and chill in the refrigerator overnight.
Remove the charlotte from the mould and serve very cold.
If you like you can decorate the charlotte with sifted cocoa powder just before serving and serve with custard.
You could also flavour the chocolate mousse with the grated rind of an unwaxed orange.

Chocolate charlotte

Raspberry Swiss roll

THIS CAKE NEVER FAILS TO IMPRESS. If you follow the recipe in stages you'll find it easy to make. You can of course use different jams for the filling.

Serves 4
Preparation time: 15 minutes
Cooking time: 15 minutes

1 Swiss roll tin approximately 30 x 23 cm (12 x 9 inches)

20 g (¾ oz) butter for greasing the tin
3 eggs
120 g (4½ oz) caster sugar
30 g (1 oz) plain flour
50 g (2 oz) cornflour
1 pinch of salt
1 350 g (12 oz) jar raspberry jam
icing sugar for decoration

Preheat the oven to 150°C (300°F) Gas Mark 2. Grease the tin and line it with greaseproof paper. Separate the eggs. Put the whites in a large bowl. Combine the yolks with the sugar in a basin. Beat until the mixture turns pale and frothy. Add the flour and cornflour and mix well.

Add the pinch of salt to the egg whites and, with a whisk, beat until they form stiff peaks. Gently fold them into the yolk-sugar mixture using a spatula.
Pour the mixture into the tin. If necessary smooth the top with a spatula to ensure even distribution. Put in the oven to cook for about 15 minutes.
As soon as it comes out of the oven, turn the sponge out onto a damp cloth and roll it up quickly in the cloth. Then unroll it and spread with a layer of raspberry jam. Roll up again in the cloth as tightly as possible. Leave to cool.
Remove the cloth, dust the cake with a little icing sugar and serve.

Yuletide chocolate log

NOWADAYS YOU CAN BUY THESE IN CAKE SHOPS. There's just one problem: you miss out on the pleasure
– and the satisfaction – of making your own Christmas cake.

Serves 6–8
Preparation time: 45 minutes
Cooking time: 20 minutes

1 baking sheet lined with greaseproof paper

For the sponge

125 g (4½ oz) caster sugar
175 g (6 oz) ground almonds
45 g (2 oz) plain flour
4 whole eggs + 5 whites
30 g (1 oz) salted butter (at room temperature), cubed
1 pinch of salt
50 g (2 oz) chopped hazelnuts
icing sugar

For the syrup

80 g (3 oz) caster sugar
80 ml (3 fl oz) water
50 ml (2 fl oz) rum

For the chocolate ganache

300 ml (10 fl oz) single cream
400 g (14 oz) dark chocolate, grated
300 ml (10 fl oz) single cream
80 g (3 oz) butter (at room temperature), cubed

Preheat the oven to 210°C (410°F) Gas Mark 6–7. Using your electric mixer (or a hand whisk), combine the sugar, ground almonds, flour, whole eggs and cubed butter.

Add the salt to the egg whites and beat them to form stiff peaks. Fold into the sponge mixture using a spatula.

Spread the mixture on the baking sheet. Sprinkle the chopped hazelnuts on top. Cook for 5–8 minutes.

Meanwhile make the syrup: slowly melt the sugar in the water and rum in a small heavy-based saucepan. Moisten the sponge with this syrup using a pastry brush.

Next make the ganache: pour the cream into a heavy-based saucepan, bring to the boil and pour it onto the grated chocolate. Stir with a spoon then add the cubed butter and mix until completely smooth.

Spread a layer of ganache over the sponge and roll up. Spread ganache on the top. Use a fork to make streaks on the chocolate.

Dust with a little icing sugar.

Twelfth Night cake with frangipane

According to tradition, whoever gets the slice containing the dried bean becomes king and may choose a queen (or vice versa).

Serves 4–6
Preparation time: 15 minutes
Cooking time: 25 minutes

1 baking sheet lined with greaseproof paper

2 sheets ready-made puff pastry
130 g (4 ½ oz) caster sugar
100 g (4 oz) salted butter (at room temperature), cubed
3 whole eggs + 1 yolk
few drops of vanilla extract
60 g (2 oz) plain flour
150 g (5 oz) ground almonds
1 dried bean

Preheat the oven to 210°C (410°F) Gas Mark 6–7.
First make the frangipane: beat the sugar and cubed butter until the mixture turns pale and slightly frothy. Add the whole eggs one at a time, while continuing to beat. Then add the vanilla extract.
Combine the flour and ground almonds in a bowl and add them to the butter-sugar-egg mixture.
Roll out one sheet of puff pastry. Spread it with the frangipane, leaving a margin of about 3 cm (1¼ inches).
Put the dried bean in the frangipane.
Moisten the edges of the pastry with a little water then cover with the other sheet of puff pastry, pressing the edges together neatly with your fingers.
Glaze the top of the cake with beaten egg yolk and make a criss-cross pattern with the point of a knife. Take care not to pierce the pastry.
Cook for about 25 minutes.
Now all you have to do is find the king!

Fruit desserts and puddings

Apples baked with honey and spices

Serves 6
Preparation time: 15 minutes
Cooking time: 35 minutes

1 gratin dish

6 apples
6 teaspoons honey
20 g (¾ oz) butter
1 pinch ground nutmeg
1 pinch ground cinnamon
2 tablespoons water

Preheat the oven to 180°C (350°F) Gas Mark 4. Wash the apples and dry them thoroughly with a clean towel. Take out the cores and pips using an apple corer or a knife. Put the apples in a dish and pour 1 teaspoon of honey over each. Put a knob of butter into each cavity and dust with the nutmeg and cinnamon. Pour 2 tablespoons of water into the bottom of the dish and cook for about 35 minutes.
Baste the apples frequently with their cooking liquid to prevent them drying out.
Serve warm or cold.

You could pour half a glass of white wine (such as a Gewürztraminer) into the dish with the water. In cooking the wine becomes concentrated and gives the syrup a delicious flavour.

TIP • Preferably use cooking apples.

Harvest pie

Serves 6
Preparation time: 20 minutes
Cooking time: 40 minutes

1 baking sheet lined with greaseproof paper

500 g (1 lb 2 oz) shortcrust pastry (see page 14)
2 kg (4 lb 8 oz) firm pears
juice of 1 lemon
60 g (2 oz) golden caster sugar
2 pinches root ginger, freshly grated
1 egg yolk

Peel and halve the pears; remove the cores and pips. Cut into thick slices. Sprinkle with lemon juice.
Mix the sugar and ginger together in a bowl. Pour this mixture over the pears and mix gently using your fingers, to give an even distribution.
Roll out the pastry to make a circle about 40 cm (14 inches) in diameter on the baking sheet. Arrange the slices of pear over half the pastry, leaving a 2 cm (¾ inch) margin. Fold the other half of the pastry over the pears and seal the edges, using your fingers to make a hem.
Whisk the egg yolk in a bowl and use it to glaze the surface of the pastry.
Cook in the oven for about 40 minutes.

TIP • You can just as easily use apples instead of pears.

Apples baked with honey and spices

Caramelized apples

Serves 4–6
Preparation time: 25 minutes
Cooking time: 35 minutes

1 charlotte mould or glass bowl, or individual moulds

20 g (¾ oz) butter for greasing the mould
100 g (4 oz) caster sugar + 50 g (2 oz) for the caramel
2 tablespoons water + 1 teaspoon boiling water + 1 glass water
2–3 drops vinegar
1.5 kg (3 lb 5 oz) apples
½ teaspoon ground cinnamon
3 eggs

Preheat the oven to 180°C (350°F) Gas Mark 4. Grease the mould with butter.
Slowly dissolve 50 g (2 oz) of sugar with 2 tablespoons of water in a heavy-based saucepan. When the mixture turns golden, add 2 or 3 drops of vinegar and take the pan off the heat. Add 1 teaspoon boiling water and stir.
Pour this caramel into the mould, tipping and turning the mould in order to coat the sides and base. Leave to cool then butter the inside of the mould where not coated with caramel.
Peel and quarter the apples; remove the cores and pips. Add a glass of water to the pan and cook them in a heavy-based saucepan on a high heat. Stir frequently to reduce the liquid, then take off the heat and add 100 g (4 oz) sugar and the cinnamon. Stir well. While the apples are still warm add the eggs one at a time, beating constantly. Pour this mixture into the caramelized mould. Cook in a bain-marie: half fill a roasting pan with boiling water, stand the mould in the water and cook in the oven for about 15–20 minutes. Leave to cool and take out of the mould just before serving.

Apple and caramel compote

It can't be overemphasized: for a good compote you need good quality fruit! No windfalls and no bruised or damaged fruit!

Serves 6
Preparation time: 15 minutes
Cooking time: 50 minutes

600 g (1 lb 5 oz) caster sugar
1 glass water
2 kg (4 lb 8 oz) cooking apples
20 ml (1 fl oz) calvados
1 small pot double cream

Slowly dissolve 200 g (7 oz) of sugar in a glass of water in a heavy-based saucepan, stirring with a spatula until the mixture turns golden brown. Remove the pan from the heat.
Peel and quarter the apples; remove the cores and pips. Mix them with the remaining sugar then put the quartered apples in the pan and cook very slowly, stirring frequently to prevent burning. You can add a tablespoon of water if they dry out too much.
Blend the cooked compote in your food processor to make it smoother. Pour in the calvados and leave to cool.
Serve the apple and caramel compote very cold with a dollop of cream.

Apple and caramel compote

Bread pudding with red fruit

Serves 4–6
Preparation time: 10 minutes
Cooking time: 8 minutes

2 eggs
50 g (2 oz) icing sugar
500 ml (just under 1 pint) milk
2 knobs of butter
1 tablespoon cooking oil
8 thick slices of stale white bread (or brioche)
300 g (10 oz) red fruit (strawberries, redcurrants, blackcurrants etc.)

Break the eggs into a shallow dish, add the sugar and beat with a fork.
Pour the milk into a deep-sided dish.
Heat 1 knob of butter and 1 tablespoon of cooking oil in a frying pan.
Quickly dip the slices of bread in the milk and then in the beaten egg and put them in the frying pan. Let them brown a little then turn them over.
Heat the other knob of butter in another frying pan, tip in the red fruit and heat slowly while stirring.
Serve the bread pudding with the red fruit and a dusting of icing sugar.

Summer pudding

Serves 4–6
Preparation time: 20 minutes
Cooking time: 5 minutes
Chill overnight

1 charlotte mould or glass bowl

400 g (14 oz) raspberries
150 g (5 oz) redcurrants
150 g (5 oz) blackberries
150 g (5 oz) caster sugar
8–10 slices brioche (or white bread)
20 g (¾ oz) butter

Grease the mould.
Quickly rinse the fruit under cold running water and drain.
Put it in a pan with the sugar and bring to the boil. Leave to simmer for about 5 minutes.
Press the slices of bread against the sides and base of the mould. Put the red fruit into the mould, filling it to the top. Keep any leftover fruit for decoration. Then cover with bread.
Put a small plate on top and place something heavy on top of the plate to weigh it down.
Leave the pudding in the refrigerator overnight.
To serve, turn it out on to a serving plate and decorate with the leftover fruit and a little cream.

Bread pudding with red fruit

Lemon pudding

Serves 4–6
Preparation time: 10 minutes
Cooking time: 30 minutes

1 deep dish about 22 cm (9 inches) in diameter

20 g (¾ oz) butter for greasing the dish
4 eggs
180 g (6 oz) caster sugar
2 heaped teaspoons vanilla sugar
500 g (1 lb 2 oz) fromage frais
grated rind of 1 lemon
1 pinch of salt

Preheat the oven to 170°C (335°F) Gas Mark 3–4.
Grease the dish with the butter.
Separate the eggs. Beat the egg yolks with the
caster sugar and the vanilla sugar until the
mixture turns creamy. Add the fromage frais and
the grated lemon rind.
Add the pinch of salt to the egg whites and beat
with a whisk to form stiff peaks. Gently fold them
into the egg yolk-sugar mixture.
Spread the mixture in the dish and cook for about
30 minutes. Leave the pudding to cool in the dish
and serve cold.

Rice cake

Serves 4
Preparation time: 5 minutes
Cooking time: 1 hour 10 minutes

1 ovenproof pudding basin

250 g (9 oz) round-grain rice
2 litres (3½ pints) milk
1 vanilla pod
80 g (3 oz) caster sugar + 50 g (2 oz) for the
caramel
4 egg yolks
3 tablespoons water
1 drop of lemon juice

Quickly wash the rice under cold running water.
Pour the milk into a heavy-based saucepan and
add the vanilla pod split in two lengthways. Bring
to the boil and pour in the rice.
Cover and leave to simmer for about 35 minutes.
Five minutes before the end of the cooking time,
add 80 g (3 oz) sugar and stir well. When done,
remove the vanilla pod, pour the rice into a basin,
pour in the egg yolks and mix well.
Preheat the oven to 180°C (350°F) Gas Mark 4.
Dissolve 50 g (2 oz) sugar in 3 tablespoons of
water in a heavy-based saucepan and cook,
stirring with a spatula until the mixture turns
golden. Remove the saucepan from the heat, add
a drop of lemon juice and stir once.
Pour the caramel into the mould and swirl it
round to coat the sides, then add the cooked rice.
Bake in the oven for about 35 minutes. The top
of the pudding should turn an attractive amber
colour.
Allow to cool before turning it out of the dish.

Prunes in red wine and cinnamon

A quick dessert that can be made in advance. It'll
take a weight off your mind!

Serves 4–6
Preparation time: 35 minutes
Cooking time 10 minutes

800 g (1 lb 12 oz) prunes
50 ml (2 fl oz) brandy
1 vanilla pod
1.5 litres (2½ pints) red wine
120 g (4½ oz) caster sugar
1 cinnamon stick
1 clove
1 pinch of ground ginger

Put the prunes and brandy in a large bowl to soak
for half an hour.
Split the vanilla pod lengthways.
Put the wine, sugar, cinnamon stick, vanilla pod,
clove and ground ginger in a heavy-based
saucepan. Bring to the boil and add the prunes
together with any liquid from the bottom of the
bowl.
Bring to the boil again and leave to simmer for
another 5 minutes.
Then take off the heat and leave the prunes to
cool in their spicy syrup.
This dish tastes even better if made the day
before.

Rice pudding

A very easy recipe that can be enhanced with
grated orange or lemon rind.

Serves 4
Preparation time: 5 minutes
Cooking time: 45 minutes

250 g (9 oz) round-grain rice
2 litres (3½ pints) milk
1 vanilla pod
80 g (3 oz) caster sugar

Quickly wash the rice in cold water. Put the milk
into a heavy-based saucepan and add the vanilla
pod split lengthways. Bring to the boil and pour
in the rice. Cover and simmer for about 45
minutes. Five minutes before the end of cooking,
add the sugar and stir well. When cooked,
remove the vanilla pod, pour the rice into a basin
and leave to cool at room temperature.

TIP • Do not stir the rice during the cooking
process.

Chocolate mousse

The dessert that everyone adores. You can also use this mousse to fill meringues, pancakes or a charlotte case.

Serves 4–6
Preparation time: 10 minutes
Cooking time: 8 minutes

Individual ramekin dishes or a large bowl

200 g (7 oz) dark chocolate
6 fresh eggs
70 g (3 oz) icing sugar
1 pinch of salt

Break the chocolate into pieces.
Heat some water in a saucepan. Put the chocolate in a bowl with a tablespoon of water and stand the bowl in the saucepan. Slowly melt the chocolate. The water should not be allowed to boil, just simmer. Take the bowl of chocolate off the heat and stir with a spoon.
Separate the eggs. Mix the egg yolks and the sugar and pour this mixture into the melted chocolate.
Add the salt to the egg whites and beat to form stiff peaks using an electric mixer (or a hand whisk). Gently fold them into the eggs-sugar-chocolate mixture, using a spatula to ensure that the egg whites are thoroughly blended, taking care not to let them break down.
Divide the mixture between the ramekin dishes. Cover with clingfilm and put the mousse in the refrigerator for about 2 hours.
Serve cold.

TIP • You can flavour the mousse with 1 tablespoon of brandy or rum and serve with Cats' tongues (Langues de chat) (see page 38).

Chocolate fondant

Serves 4–6
Preparation time: 10 minutes
Cooking time: 8 minutes
Make the day before

1 soufflé dish or charlotte mould, greased with butter

350g (12 oz) dark chocolate
1 tablespoon water
4 eggs
175 g (6 oz) butter (at room temperature), cubed + 20 g (¾ oz) for greasing the dish
100 g (4 oz) caster sugar
1 pinch of salt

Grease the dish with butter.
Break the chocolate into pieces.
Heat some water in a saucepan. Put the chocolate in a bowl with a tablespoon of water and stand the bowl in the saucepan. Slowly melt the chocolate. The water should not be allowed to boil, just simmer.
Separate the eggs.
Mix the butter and sugar in a bowl until the mixture turns creamy. Then pour in the melted chocolate, mix well and add the egg yolks one at a time, stirring continuously.
Add the salt to the egg whites and beat them to form stiff peaks using an electric mixer (or a hand whisk). Fold them gently into the eggs-sugar-chocolate mixture using a spatula to ensure that the egg whites are thoroughly blended, taking care not to let them break down.
Pour the mixture into the dish.
Cover the top with clingfilm and refrigerate overnight.
Remove from the dish just before serving. It should be eaten very cold.
You may wish to dust the fondant with icing sugar.

Chocolate fondant

Almond filling

You'll want to dip your finger in this, like a child! You can use it as a base for tarts, especially ones made with cherries or other stone fruit. During cooking the almond cream absorbs the flavour of the fruit and helps to keep the pastry crisp.

Serves 4–6
Preparation time: 10 minutes

150 g (5 oz) butter, at room temperature, cubed
120 g (4½ oz) icing sugar
3 eggs
150 g (5 oz) ground almonds
50 g (2 oz) plain flour

Mix the butter and icing sugar together in a large bowl with a whisk. As soon as the mixture turns pale, add the eggs one at a time and stir.
Then pour in the ground almonds, mix well and add the flour.
The hardest part is done: just keep it in the refrigerator until you want to use it.

Orange and almond gratin

A very sophisticated dish but one that is nevertheless easy to make. You can use the same basic recipe to make strawberry or peach gratins, etc.

Serves 4
Preparation time: 25 minutes
Cooking time: 10 minutes

1 small gratin dish

3 oranges
40 g (1½ oz) butter (at room temperature), cubed + 20 g (¾ oz) for greasing the dish
80 g (3 oz) icing sugar
80 g (3 oz) ground almonds
1 egg
100 ml (4 fl oz) whipping cream

Grease the dish with butter.
Wash and dry the oranges. Remove the peel and cut the oranges into thick slices. Carefully remove the white pith.
Preheat the grill section of your oven to 210°C (410°F) Gas Mark 6–7.
Make the almond cream: put the cubed butter in a large bowl. Pour in the icing sugar and ground almonds; mix well.
Add the egg and mix again.
Pour the cream into another bowl and whip vigorously. Pour the whipped cream into the almond cream mixture and blend until smooth.
Pour the almond cream into the dish and arrange the orange slices on top. Grill for about 10 minutes.
Leave to cool a little and serve warm.

Chestnut spread

Sufficient for filling 1 sponge cake or 10 meringues

Preparation time: 10 minutes

300 g (10 oz) tinned chestnut purée
½ vanilla pod
3–4 tablespoons caster sugar

Scrape the seeds out of the vanilla pod and discard the pod. Blend the ingredients in a food processor. Chill in the refrigerator until you want to use it. Use to fill a sponge cake or meringues.

Orange and almond gratin

Floating islands

Serves 4–6
Preparation time: 10 minutes
Cooking time: 3 minutes

8 egg whites
1 pinch of salt
custard (see page 18)

Heat a large saucepan of water.
Put the egg whites in a large bowl, add the pinch
of salt and beat with an electric whisk to form
stiff peaks.
When the water is boiling, carefully place
spoonfuls of egg white in the water. Lower the
heat and leave to cook for 3 minutes.
Use a skimmer to lift out the egg whites, drain
them and float them on top of the custard.
You may like to pour a little caramel over the egg
whites.

Baked custard

See page 18 for recipe

Egg custard

Serves 4–6
Preparation time: 10 minutes
Cooking time: 30 minutes

1 ovenproof gratin dish

1 litre (1¾ pints) milk
200 g (7 oz) caster sugar
1 vanilla pod
6 eggs

Preheat the oven to 150°C (300°F) Gas Mark 2.
Put the milk in a heavy-based saucepan with the
sugar and vanilla pod, split in two lengthways.
Bring to the boil. Whisk the eggs in a large bowl
and gradually pour them into the boiling milk,
stirring all the time. Then pour the eggs and milk
into a mould.
Place the mould in a deep dish two-thirds full of
boiling water (a bain-marie). Cook in the oven for
about 30 minutes.
Serve warm in the dish in which it was cooked.
You can flavour the egg custard with the grated
rind of half a lemon.

Floating islands

Table of recipes

Table of recipes

Acknowledgments

A big thanks to Elio, his father and mother, for the photo on page 27 and to Marie-Monique for the use of her house.
Thanks too to Akiko and Pierre for their patience.
For trying out the recipes: Ilona Chovankova

Shopping and household items

Maison de Famille, 10 place de la Madeleine, 75008 Paris
for pages 39 (bowl), 45 (plate, top left), 53 and 71 (plate and cake dish), 77, 84, 97, 101, 119, 121, 131, 139, 140, 146 and 155.

ISBN 1-84430-034-X

Printed in Singapore by Tien Wah Press